Instant AutoCAD®

Architectural Desktop 3.3

Instant AutoCAD®
Architectural Desktop 3.3

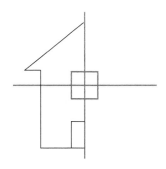

Stephen J. Ethier
Christine A. Ethier

CADInnovations

PEARSON

Prentice
Hall

Upper Saddle River, New Jersey
Columbus, Ohio

Library of Congress Cataloging-in-Publication Data

Ethier, Stephen J.
   Instant AutoCAD: architectural desktop 3.3 / Stephen J. Ethier, Christine A. Ethier.
      p.   cm.
   Includes index.
   ISBN 0-13-111106-X
   1. Architectural design--Programmed instruction. 2. Architectural
drawing--Computer-aided design. 3. AutoCAD. I. Ethier, Christine A. II. Title.

NA2728.E8423 2005
720'.28'402855369--dc21   2002032254

Executive Editor: Debbie Yarnell
Managing Editor: Judy Casillo
Production Editor: Louise N. Sette
Production Supervision: Lisa Garboski, *bookworks*
Design Coordinator: Diane Ernsberger
Cover Designer: Jason Moore
Cover Art: Stephen J. Ethier
Production Manager: Deidra Schwartz
Marketing Manager: Jimmy Stephens

This book was set in Adobe Caslon. It was printed and bound by Demand Production Center. The cover was printed by Demand Production Center.

Disclaimer:
The publication is designed to provide tutorial information about AutoCAD® and/or other Autodesk computer programs. Every effort has been made to make this publication complete and as accurate as possible. The reader is expressly cautioned to use any and all precautions necessary, and to take appropriate steps to avoid hazards, when engaging in the activities described herein.

Neither the author nor the publisher makes any representations or warranties of any kind, with respect to the materials set forth in this publication, express or implied, including without limitation any warranties of fitness for a particular purpose or merchantability. Nor shall the author or the publisher be liable for any special, consequential or exemplary damages resulting, in whole or in part, directly or indirectly, from the reader's use of, or reliance upon, this material or subsequent revisions of this material.

Pearson Education Ltd.
Pearson Education Singapore Pte. Ltd.
Pearson Education Canada, Ltd.
Pearson Education—Japan

Pearson Education Australia Pty. Limited
Pearson Education North Asia Ltd.
Pearson Educación de Mexico, S. A. de C.V.
Pearson Education Malaysia Pte. Ltd.

10 9 8 7 6 5 4 3 2 1
ISBN: 0-13-111106-X

To Mary Balser,
for her love, her understanding
and her true friendship
and to George, James,
Robbie, and Willie
for all the wonderful stories
they add to our lives and all
the smiles they inspire in Mary
with love

Preface

Instant AutoCAD: Architectural Desktop 3.3, another text in the *Instant AutoCAD* series, continues the tradition of delivering technical information in a quick and easy format. Although this book does not attempt to cover all the complexities of the program, as we're sure you can understand that a book this size can touch only on the basics, it does offer a look at architectural design in the world of Architectural Desktop, from concepts to construction documents.

Architectural Desktop (ADT) is a 3D, object-based, parametric designer with which the user initially creates 3D models of buildings from mass elements and uses this conceptual design to create a refined building system. Construction documents can then be created. Architectural Desktop is fully integrated and makes use of the AutoCAD graphic interface. The power of the program lies in the object-oriented facilities that can alter an existing design for use in a variety of applications. The architectural objects are able to relate intelligently with one another. At any time you can change the shape and size of the objects that make up the design. Once a design has been created, two-dimensional drawings, in various views, can be created automatically, applying drafting standards for dimensioning and symbol application.

The aim of this text is to give you information and hands-on practical experience so that you will be able to make use of this complex interface in the most efficient manner possible. *Instant AutoCAD: Architectural Desktop 3.3* contains hundreds of figures to illustrate the various processes needed to move from a concept to a fully annotated drawing using a 3D model as the base. For each new process, concise theory is presented followed by a practical application to reinforce the newly obtained information.

The layout of the book is explained in Chapter 1, but it is essential to understand the various components of a chapter. The first section in each chapter lists key ideas that will be covered in that chapter. Throughout the chapter you may see a variety of elements: stylized print lifting an idea from the pages for emphasis, tip boxes that stress a certain fact about the program, command sequences in very simple print that present the desired user's input in bold letters, and hands-on exercises to reinforce a new idea. At the end of each chapter you'll find a short-answer test, a series of questions that require longer answers, and a number of assignments. Remember that the more effort you put into study and exercise completion, the more you'll take away from the text in learning. It's up to you.

An Integrated Learning Assistant is available for this text @ www.viziwiz.com.

Architectural Desktop is a very complex and powerful program, but the experience of learning it shouldn't be dull or threatening. Rather, the many exercises, the informal language, and the friendly graphics will make it easier to learn. The topics that cover the most basic operations are explained more fully, whereas others are left for you to investigate on your own. We're sure this is the start of a journey that will bring wider horizons, lucrative results, and the pleasure that comes with mastery of a new tool.

Acknowledgments

First of all, many thanks to Stephen Helba, friend and fellow movie buff, for his tireless work on our behalf; to Debbie Yarnell, our Executive Editor, for her capable mind and phenomenal adaptability; to Michelle Churma, our technical editor, for her dedicated expertise; and to Bubba and Goblin, for their calming and grounding influence on Michelle. Also, thanks to Lisa Garboski for her fine project management and to Pat Wilson for her excellent manuscript editing. In addition, we wish to thank the following reviewers: David Braun, Spokane Community College (WA); John Knapp, Metropolitan Community College (IA); and Bert A. Siebold, Ph.D, Murray State University (KY).

And, of course, to Autodesk, for their ever-prompt technical support and knowledge, we are always grateful.

Contents

Instant AutoCAD®
Architectural Desktop 3.3

Chapter 1

Introduction to Architectural Desktop

The Plan

The British Museum model for the new Great Court is displayed inside the museum. Throughout the world, architectural plans, renderings, models, and 3D walk-throughs indicate the near and the distant future of the world's architecture.

Key Concepts

◆ Architectural Desktop Design Process
◆ Interacting with Architectural Desktop
◆ Display System
◆ Drawing Setup

Welcome!

Welcome to *Instant AutoCAD: Architectural Desktop 3.3*. If you're familiar with other books in the *Instant AutoCAD* series, then you're already aware that we want to teach you how to use Architectural Desktop in the fastest and most effective way possible. We want you to start using Architectural Desktop right away, so that your confidence grows as quickly as your knowledge.

Architectural Desktop (ADT) is a 3D, object-based, parametric designer. You can initially create 3D models of buildings from mass elements and then use this conceptual design to create a refined building system. You can then create construction documents. Figure 1.1 shows the design progression in a simplified form.

Architectural Desktop is designed to operate inside AutoCAD. In fact, it's fully integrated and makes use of the AutoCAD graphic interface. However, it contains additional pull-down menus and toolbars that are specific to architectural design. Before attempting to use Architectural Desktop, you should be familiar with the basics of drawing in Auto-CAD. If you are unfamiliar with standard AutoCAD, you should start with the *Instant AutoCAD: Essentials* text. It will instruct you in all the basics of using AutoCAD and will allow you to glide smoothly into using Architectural Desktop and this text.

In this chapter you'll be introduced to the Architectural Desktop design process, and you'll practice interacting with Architectural Desktop pull-down menus, toolbars, and the DesignCenter. Let the tour begin!

**Before attempting to use Architectural Desktop,
you should be familiar with the basics of
drawing in AutoCAD.**

A Brief Tour

Our goal is to provide you with background knowledge of Architectural Desktop commands as well as to teach you the practical applications of its features. The majority of commands or procedures introduced are followed by hands-on, practical applications. Although this hands-on approach is essential for physical learners, the concrete tasks are beneficial experiences for relational and mental learners as well.

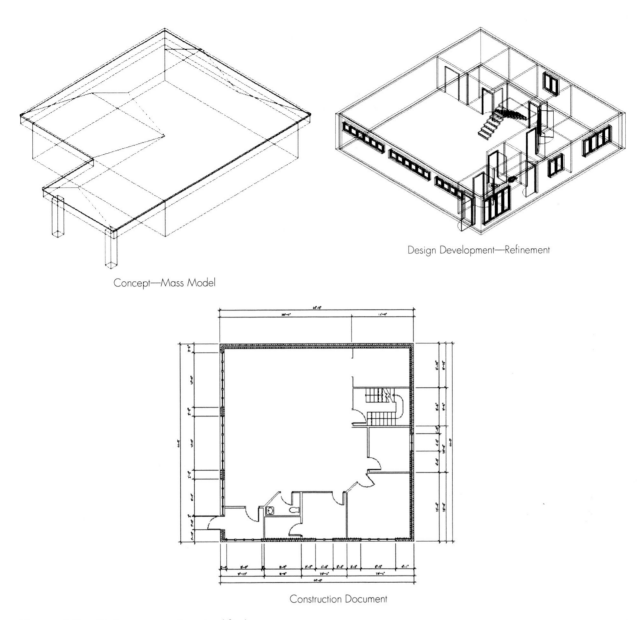

Concept—Mass Model

Design Development—Refinement

Construction Document

Figure 1.1 Design progression simplified

 The hands-on sections are easily identified by the **Hands-On** heading. Any time you see **the hand**, you'll know it's time to practice using Architectural Desktop.

 You'll also notice **icons** in the left margin. These icons represent Architectural Desktop commands that are picked from menus and help you to identify the actual commands in the program.

 The **lightbulb/idea** symbol is attached to the Tip boxes throughout the text; these boxes provide tips on items that help you avoid beginner pitfalls.

Your CD-ROM includes numerous models and drawings to make learning easier and faster. Be sure to copy those into the IAADT3 folder (subdirectory) on your computer. (Go to Appendix A if you need help making your copy.)

The end of each chapter provides you with questions and assignments to reinforce what you've learned.

Architectural Desktop Design Process

To create in 3D you must understand some basic concepts and terms. To help you understand them, let's review the Architectural Desktop design process. As you read through this text you will build on these concepts, going into greater detail. For now, familiarize yourself with the following basic principles.

Conceptual Design

The design process starts with the concept. To assist the designer, Architectural Desktop has objects called *mass elements*. These are predefined basic shapes. You assemble these basic shapes to create the conceptual exterior layout. This type of layout is referred to as a *balloon layout* when performed in 2D. In Architectural Desktop, the objects are three-dimensional. You can link these 3D elements into a single complex object called a *mass group*. Figure 1.2 shows mass elements and a mass group.

Spatial Design

Once you have completed the conceptual exterior design, you then start space planning. You can create building floorplates (horizontal cross sections) by slicing the building at various elevations. From these floorplates, you can define the spaces that will be used to create walls. Figure 1.3 shows floorplates and space boundaries.

Design Development

Once you have created the preliminary floor plan from the mass model, you start to refine the design by adding more detail and developing a more explicit layout. This involves specifying wall styles, placing column grids, and adding components such as roofs. Figure 1.4 shows a plan with added wall styles.

Refine the design by adding more detail and developing a more explicit layout.

Object Driven

Every object you create using the Architectural Desktop tools contains an inherent intelligence. A wall knows it's a wall, a door knows it's a door, and so on. Because of this intelli-

Figure 1.2 (a) Mass elements and (b) a mass group

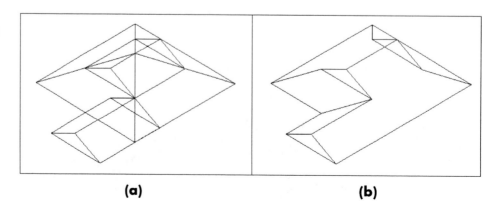

(a)   (b)

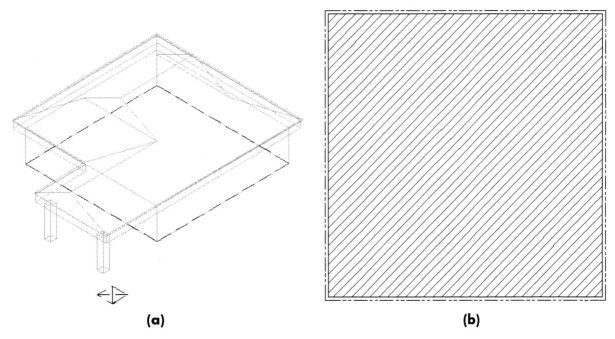

(a)   **(b)**

Figure 1.3 (a) Floorplates and (b) space boundaries

Figure 1.4 Design development of floor plan

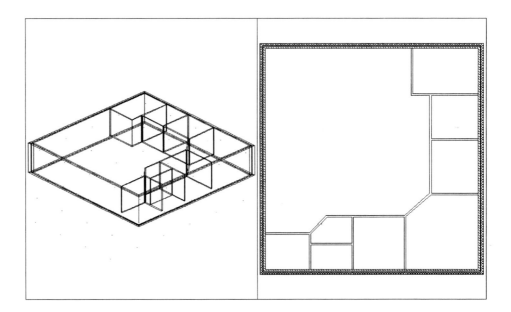

gence, you can place objects next to each other, and the objects know how to interact. For example, when a door is placed in a wall, the wall automatically cuts itself to allow the insertion. This is where the power of object-driven Architectural Desktop is displayed. However, there is a price to pay. The objects are now not just simple lines but sophisticated components. Consequently, you will need to learn how to manipulate these components efficiently.

Each of the various intelligent objects is a true 3D model. Using these you can create a complete three-dimensional model that can be viewed in a variety of ways including plan, elevation, section, and perspective. Figure 1.5 shows a partial plan, and Figure 1.6 shows a 3D view of the same model.

Figure 1.5 Two-dimensional view (plan) of 3D model

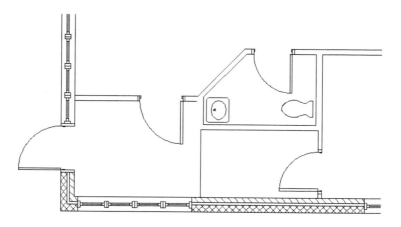

Figure 1.6 Three-dimensional view of 3D model

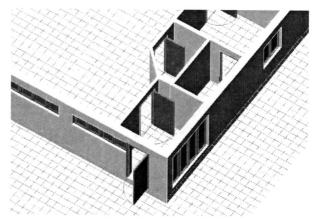

Construction Documentation

Once the design of the building is complete, construction drawings can be created. Various automatic dimensioning techniques can be used, and standard symbols such as door and window tags can be applied. Schedule tables can be created also and updated automatically if an object is added or deleted from the design. Figure 1.7 shows a partial plan with dimensions.

Figure 1.7 Partial construction document showing dimensions

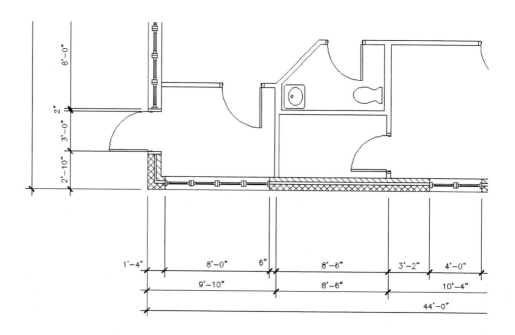

Advanced Features

A number of advanced features such as Layout tools, Masking, and Anchors can be used to enhance your design. These are not covered in the main body of this text, but some information about them is included in the appendices.

Autodesk
Architectural
Desktop 3.3

Hands-On: Navigating the Menus and Toolbars

1.   Start Architectural Desktop 3.3 by:

a.   locating the ADT3.3 shortcut icon and double-clicking it

or

b.   picking the Windows™ Start button, entering the Programs submenu, finding the Architectural Desktop 3.3 menu, and picking the Architectural Desktop 3.3 menu item.

2.   A Start Up dialog box may appear in the center of the screen. Depending on your setup, your Start Up dialog box may be the traditional version or the newer *Today* version. This is controlled in the Options dialog box, under the System Tab, in the General Options section. In either case, start a new drawing using Start from Scratch set to English units. This will give you a blank drawing file from which to start. Now you're able to roam freely around the Architectural Desktop screen (see Figure 1.8).

3.   Get to know the layout of the Architectural Desktop screen. Look at your screen and the following text, but do not exit Architectural Desktop.

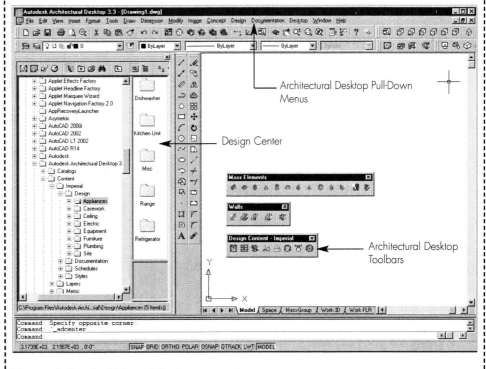

Figure 1.8   Architectural Desktop screen layout

TIP: Using Standard AutoCAD

You can use the standard stand-alone version of AutoCAD to open Architectural Desktop drawings. Also, you can view and plot them. The only limitation is that you cannot edit them parametrically. Anyone currently running AutoCAD 2000 or above can install the AEC Object Enabler to load drawings and access the AEC objects created using AutoCAD Architectural Desktop. This can be downloaded from Autodesk's Point A Internet site.

Interacting with Architectural Desktop

When you start Architectural Desktop, four additional pull-down menus are added to the standard AutoCAD pull-down menus. There's also a new menu group called AECARCHX that gives you access to new Architectural Desktop toolbars. Figure 1.8 shows the screen layout. Some of the Architectural Desktop toolbars have been displayed. The DesignCenter on the left is also open.

Toolbars

There are 38 Architectural Desktop toolbars that can be used to access commands throughout the design and documentation phases. To access these toolbars, right-click on any displayed Architectural toolbar, or right-click in an open gray space in the top toolbar area. A context menu will appear, allowing you to open or close any toolbar, as shown partially in Figure 1.9. The Architectural Desktop toolbars are located under the AECARCHX menu group.

Pull-Down Menus

You should first familiarize yourself with the contents of the four new pull-down menus. Their headings are Concept, Design, Documentation, and Desktop. These deal solely with Architectural Desktop. Figure 1.10 shows the contents of the pull-down menus.

Figure 1.9   Access to Architectural Desktop toolbars

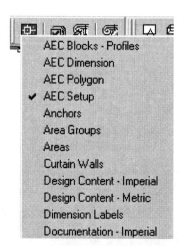

Figure 1.10   Architectural Desktop pull-down menus

Hands-On: Moving About the Screen

1.   Architectural Desktop should be on your screen with the Start Up dialog box closed. You're going to practice moving around the screen and accessing commands.

2.   Open the Concept pull-down menu and review the list of menu items as shown in Figure 1.10. All these items relate to the creation of a concept 3D model.

3.   Pick the Concept/Show Model Explorer pull-down menu item and observe what happens. A special viewer is displayed, as shown in Figure 1.11. This viewer is used to view the 3D model. Close the viewer.

4.   Let's take a look at what's inside some of the other pull-down menus. Open the Design pull-down menu and review the listed menu items. Move the cursor and stop on the Walls heading. A cascading menu should appear, as shown in Figure 1.12(a). All these items relate to the addition, creation, and modification of wall objects.

Figure 1.11   Model Explorer viewer

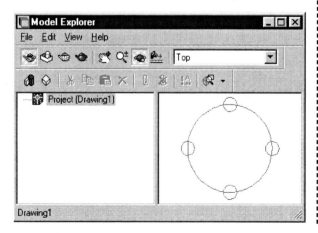

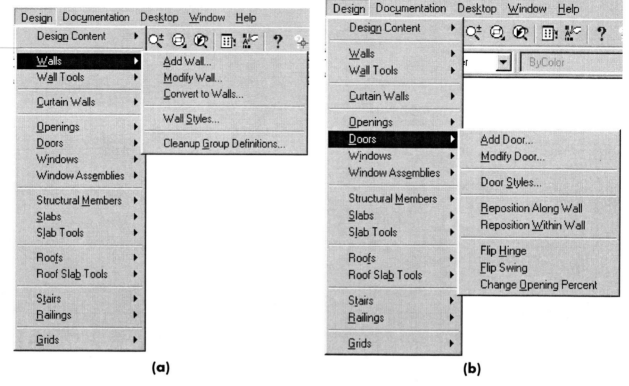

(a)   **(b)**

Figure 1.12   Design pull-down menu showing Walls and Doors menus

Move the cursor farther down the Design menu and rest it on the Doors item. Another cascading menu will appear, as shown in Figure 1.12(b). These items are used to add and manipulate door objects in the design.

Open the Documentation pull-down menu and review its contents. These items refer to the application of symbols or markers to a drawing.

Move your cursor down and rest it on the Schedule Tags heading. The cascading menu will appear. You can see that it contains various tags that can be added to the drawing to indicate item numbers that refer to doors, windows, and other objects.

Open the Desktop pull-down menu. It contains various options that apply to the whole design, as opposed to one of the three distinct phases of the design process.

5.   Now, let's look at some of the Architectural Desktop toolbars. Pick Toolbars from the View pull-down menu. When the Toolbars tab of the Customize dialog box appears, set the Menu Group to AECARCHX, as shown in Figure 1.13. This gives you access to the various Architectural Desktop toolbars.

Check the Mass Elements box so that the Mass Elements toolbar appears. These are objects that you'll use initially to create a 3D concept model. Now, close the Toolbars dialog box, but leave the Mass Elements toolbar visible.

Right-click on the Mass Elements toolbar. A context menu appears listing all the available Architectural Desktop toolbars. Pick on the Mass Groups menu item. The Mass Groups toolbar appears. This toolbar is used to group individual mass elements into a complex shape. We'll go into detail on this in Chapter 2.

Close the two Architectural Desktop toolbars.

The purpose of this exercise is to familiarize you with moving around the Architectural Desktop pull-down menus and toolbars. You're now going to learn more about how Architectural Desktop operates.

Figure 1.13
Toolbars tab of the
Customize dialog box
showing the AECARCHX
menu group

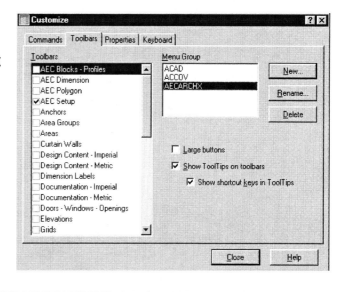

Display System

Architectural Desktop is designed around a unique, view-dependent display system. When you switch to a particular viewport, the representation of objects displayed changes, depending on the display system applied to the viewport. Thus, if you go to a Mass-Group viewport, you'll see only mass groups. If you switch to the Work-Flr layout, you'll see a two-dimensional plan representation of objects such as walls, doors, or windows. If you change your viewpoint in the Work-Flr viewport to a three-dimensional view, you'll then see the 3D representations of the architectural objects.

The representation of objects displayed will change depending on the display system applied.

In Figure 1.14 the image on the left shows a 3D view in the Work-Flr viewport. You can see the 3D elements of the stairs. The image on the right shows the same viewport but with a plan (2D) view. The stairs are now shown as simplified 2D objects. How is this accomplished? Architectural Desktop controls the visibility of layers depending on the display system applied to the viewport and the set viewpoint.

The display system is fully customizable, but thankfully the Architectural Desktop program already comes with template files for imperial and metric drawings [AEC Arch (Imperial).dwt and AEC Arch (Metric).dwt]. These template files contain all the display systems and layers ready for your use. It is very important to start your design with one of the template files. Template files are accessed when you start a new drawing and use the Template button. This text comes with a startup file (iaadt3start.dwg) that contains the settings for the imperial template file. You will be asked to use this file when starting exercises in this book.

The template files or the iaadt3start.dwg startup file for this text contains a series of layout tabs. You select the appropriate tab for the part of the design on which you're working. Figure 1.15 shows the layout tabs from the iaadt3start.dwg startup drawing.

You can see that there are tabs for different types of layouts such as Mass-Group, Space, and Work-3D. When you pick on a tab, a different viewport configuration appears. Each viewport in the configuration has a different display system applied to it. To find out what display system is applied to a viewport, activate the desired viewport

Figure 1.14   Single viewport with two different views displayed

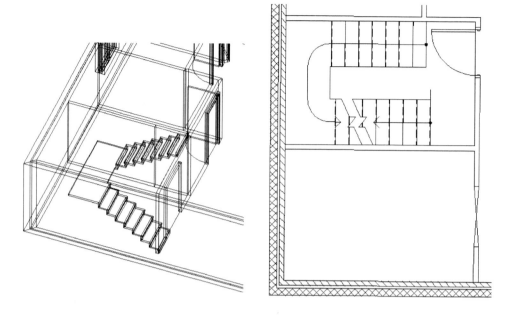

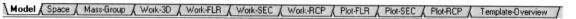

Figure 1.15   Layout tabs

Figure 1.16
Viewport Display
Configuration dialog
box

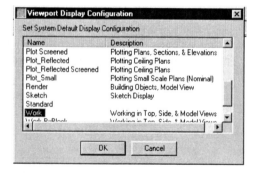

and pick Select Display from the Desktop pull-down menu. The Viewport Display Configuration dialog box appears, as shown in Figure 1.16. The highlighted name is the display system that has been applied to that viewport. If you pick on another name, that display system is applied to the viewport. Be careful not to switch a display system unintentionally. Figure 1.16 also shows the Space tab active and the Viewport Display Configuration dialog box displayed. You can see that Work is the highlighted name and therefore the display system applied to the space viewport.

Hands-On: Using the Display System and Layout Tabs

1.   Start Architectural Desktop (if you haven't done so already).

2.   Using the File/Open File pull-down menu command, open the file called ADTEX1A (IAADT3 folder). It contains a partial model for you to practice with.

3. Review the tabs at the bottom of the graphic screen. These are used to switch to different working screens. As you work on your design you can switch from tab to tab.

4. Pick the Template-Overview tab. The graphic screen switches to display a layout showing all the various viewport configurations. Zoom in on the top-right layout. This represents the Mass-Group layout. Zoom in close on the text. It lists the default settings.

You may want to plot a paper copy of the entire layout to use as a guide to the various individual layouts. It should be noted that the Template-Overview does not match the individual layouts exactly. You may notice some minor differences.

Now look at the layout tabs that run along the bottom of the screen. These coincide with the layouts in the Template-Overview. Can you see the tab marked Mass-Group? You may have to use the scroll buttons located at the left of the tabs to find it.

5. Pick the Mass-Group tab. The left viewport contains the mass elements (magenta) used in the initial design. The right viewport contains the mass groups (cyan). These are created by combining elements into a group. The objects in red represent floorplate slices. These are used to create preliminary floor plans.

6. You're now going to see what display system is applied to each of the viewports. You need to work in model space inside the viewports. To do this, make sure that the MODEL button at the bottom of the screen is depressed. The cursor can now move around in each separate viewport, allowing you access to the model. To activate a viewport's model space, pick inside the desired viewport.

Activate the left viewport by picking in open space inside the viewport. Go to the Desktop pull-down menu and pick the Select Display item. A dialog box similar to Figure 1.17 appears. Note how the name Concept_Mass is highlighted. That is the display system applied to the viewport. Review the description. It identifies what will be displayed in the viewport using that system. OK the dialog box without making any changes.

7. Activate the right viewport by picking in open space inside the viewport. Go to the Desktop pull-down menu and pick the Select Display item. A dialog box similar to Figure 1.18 appears. Note how the name Concept_Group is highlighted. That is the display system applied to the viewport. Pick the Concept_Mass name and pick OK to exit.

Note how the cyan mass groups disappeared and were replaced with the magenta mass elements. This is because you applied a different display system to the viewport.

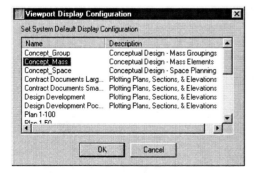

Figure 1.17 Viewport Display Configuration dialog box showing Concept_Mass

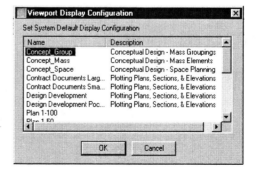

Figure 1.18 Viewport Display Configuration dialog box showing Concept_Group

Return to the Viewport Display Configuration dialog box and highlight Concept_Group. Pick OK to apply the display system. The viewport should display the cyan element groups.

8. Go through the other tabs and check each of the different displays.

Drawing Setup

As mentioned before, when you start a new design, you should always use the template files supplied with Architectural Desktop. There are 16 templates—8 imperial and 8 metric—that control various types of layouts such as model building and planning. For the beginner there are two you will concentrate on: AEC Arch (Imperial).dwt and AEC Arch (Metric).dwt. They contain all the initial settings for starting an architectural model/drawing. However, for this text you'll be using a different drawing when starting your exercises, namely, the file called iaadt2start.dwg. It contains all the settings of the AEC Arch (Imperial).dwt template file but also includes some additional specific settings for this book.

Let's review the various elements that are set up in a new drawing. Under the Desktop pull-down menu you find the Drawing Setup menu item. When picked, it displays a dialog box similar to Figure 1.19. Using this dialog box, you control the units, scale, layering, and display. Normally, these are set for you when you start with the template or startup drawing. However, you will need to adjust the scale for your particular drawing.

The next items to review are the new options added for Architectural Desktop. Under the Tools pull-down menu you find the Options menu item. The dialog box contains five new tabs for Architectural Desktop. You may need to scroll (using the double arrows to the right of the tabs) to the right to see the tabs (see Figure 1.20).

These new tabs contain settings specific to Architectural Desktop. As a beginner, you'll probably not have to make any changes to these settings. When you're more experienced, you may want to make some adjustments for your particular designs.

Figure 1.19
Drawing Setup dialog box

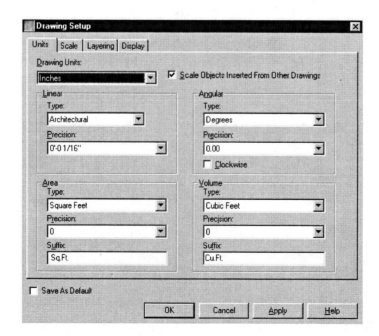

Figure 1.20
Options dialog box showing new Architectural tabs

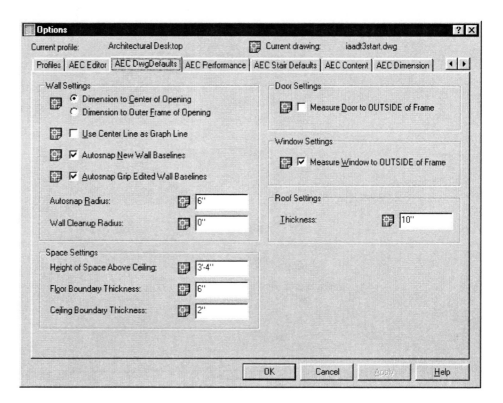

Hands-On: Reviewing Drawing Setup and Options

1.   Start Architectural Desktop if you haven't done so already.

2.   Using the File/Open File pull-down menu command, open the file called IAADT3START, which contains initial settings for your exercises (Refer to Appendix A for file location.). Use Saveas to save the drawing as EX1A.

3.   Open the Desktop pull-down menu and pick the Drawing Setup menu item. Review the settings under the Units tab. Note the Precision text box. This setting controls how small a fraction you can enter; this is important for setting text heights.

4.   Pick the Scale tab. Note that the initial scale is set to 1/4"=1'-0". Depending on your project, you may have to change this setting to match your drawing scale.

5.   Pick the Layering tab. Note the LAYER key style. This setting is used to automatically create layers as you create objects in your drawing. It has been set to AIA (American Institute of Architects) layering standards. Also note the Layer Standards/Key File. It's set when you install Architectural Desktop. It contains all the layer information. It should be normally set to:

C:\Program Files\AutoCAD Architectural 3\Content\Layers\AecLayerStd.dwg

Close the dialog box.

6.   Open the Tools pull-down menu and pick the Options menu item. Review the six new AEC tabs that are on the far right of the dialog box. You may have to scroll over to see them. Display each one in turn so that you're familiar with their content.

In a Nutshell

Architectural Desktop is a 3D, object-based, parametric designer. You have now gone over the initial design process, which involves concepts, design development, and construction documentation. You should be comfortable moving around the menus and screen and be able to open an existing drawing or start a new one.

The Display System is an extremely important part of Architectural Desktop. It is the foundation for the display of the intelligent objects you use to create your design.

Once you're ready, move on to Chapter 2.

 Testing... testing... 1, 2, 3

Fill-in-the-Blanks

1. Basic predefined shapes are called _____.

2. The design process in Architectural Desktop contains three distinct phases. They are:

   _____

   _____

   _____

Multiple Choice

3. Every object in Architectural Desktop contains:

   a.   walls

   b.   windows

   c.   doors

   d.   intelligence

   e.   all the above

4. The new Architectural Desktop toolbars are:

   a.   Concrete, Design, Documentation, and Desktop

   b.   Concept, Design, Documentation, and Desktop

   c.   Concrete, Design, Development, and Desktop

   d.   Concept, Description, Development, and Desktop

True or False

5. In Architectural Desktop, dimensions cannot be updated automatically.   T or F

6. Space planning happens in the second phase of design.   T or F

What?

1. What do you feel is the main strength of Architectural Desktop?
2. What do we mean by the term *object driven*?
3. Describe the different display systems in Architectural Desktop.
4. How can you determine which display system is active?
5. Why must you start each drawing with a template file?

Let's Get Busy!

1. Open drawing file DESIGN1A, which contains a preliminary design for you to practice on. Open the various layout tabs, noting the items displayed. Experiment with applying different display systems to the various viewports.
2. Open drawing file DESIGN1B, which contains a preliminary design for you to practice on. Open the various layout tabs, noting the items displayed. Experiment with applying different display systems to the various viewports.
3. Open drawing file DESIGN1C, which contains a preliminary design for you to practice on. Open the various layout tabs, noting the items displayed. Experiment with applying different display systems to the various viewports.

Chapter 2

Viewing and Working in 3D

Hampton Court

One of Henry VIII's favorite homes of the almost 70 from which he had to choose boasts some amazing architecture, from the many rooms of the Great Kitchen to the beautifully decorated chimneys that dot the skyline. Architecture for royalty exemplified the opulence that extreme wealth could buy in the 1400s and 1500s.

Key Concepts

- ◆ Coordinate Systems
- ◆ Planar Creation
- ◆ UCS Icon
- ◆ Shade Modes
- ◆ 3D Orbit
- ◆ Object Viewer
- ◆ UCS Working Plane

Where Are You?

The key to the creation of complex 3D designs is to be aware of your own visual orientation in relation to the model you want to create and to decide on the working planes on which the creation is going to take place. This chapter will introduce you to concepts relating to working in 3D, namely, viewing the 3D model in different ways and creating the working planes that allow you to design on any axis.

Introduction to 3D

When you reach the design development stage, most of your creation can take place on a 2D plane that will automatically generate 3D objects in their proper orientation. However, in the conceptual stage and when viewing the 3D model, you'll need to understand manipulation in 3D space. To move from two-dimensional sketches to a three-dimensional model, you need to understand some 3D concepts. This section reviews the basic concepts so that you'll be able to understand the Architectural Desktop creation process more easily.

The mental skills required to work in 3D are different from those needed for drawing in 2D. In drafting (2D), the designer translates the three-dimensional attributes of an object into flat, two-dimensional views—plan and elevation—as shown in Figure 2.1.

In modeling (3D), the designer takes into consideration all three dimensions. This sounds complicated, but actually it allows the design to be formulated faster because the user can see the entire model at any time, instead of having to work on one 2D view at a time.

The key to the creation of complex 3D designs is to be aware of your own visual orientation in relation to the model you want to create.

Figure 2.1
Transforming a 3D
object into a 2D
drawing

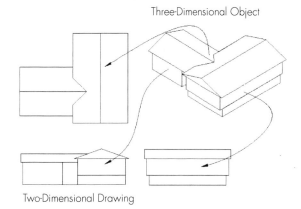

Three-Dimensional Object

Two-Dimensional Drawing

Coordinate Systems

To keep track of the three axes, there are two coordinate systems in AutoCAD: the *WCS* and the *UCS*.

WCS stands for World Coordinate System. This is AutoCAD's master coordinate system. It has X, Y, and Z coordinate axes with origin points of 0x, 0y, 0z. However, you can't change the orientation of this system or move it in any way. All dimensional information is related back to the WCS. This guarantees that you cannot get "lost" in 3D space. The WCS can always be used as a frame of reference. It always stays right where you saw it last.

UCS stands for User Coordinate System. This system has X, Y, and Z axes just like the WCS. The difference is that the UCS axes can be rotated, moved, or aligned with any location on the 3D part. You can use the UCS to create planes on which you can create your 3D design. Figure 2.2 shows a hand holding a cube. If it were your hand holding the cube, and you wanted to draw on it, all you would need to do is pick the side to draw on, get a pencil, and start to draw. The procedure is similar in Architectural Desktop. You must tell the program on what plane (side) the drawing or construction is going to take place. Once the plane is defined, you can draw anywhere on it.

Planar Creation

When you construct in three dimensions, the drawing is still based on a flat, 2D plane (planar). A plane is defined by its XY coordinates. The direction is defined by the Z axis. When you start AutoCAD, the XY plane is parallel to the screen, and the positive portion of the Z axis is pointing toward you.

To help visualize the three axes, use the right-hand rule, which is illustrated in Figure 2.3. To try it yourself, hold your right hand in front of the screen with the back of it parallel to the screen, and make a fist. Now, extend the thumb out, toward the right; it points

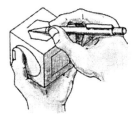

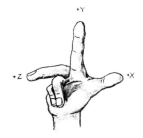

Figure 2.2
Manually drawing on
the face of a cube

Figure 2.3   The right-hand
rule for axis orientation

in the positive X direction. Extend the index (or first) finger upward; it points in the positive Y direction. Finally, extend the middle finger toward yourself; it points in the positive Z direction. If you rotate your hand in any direction, the orientations of the axes to one another remain the same. When you move your UCS around your model, the orientation of the X, Y, and Z axes remains the same.

UCS Icon

You have probably noticed the UCS icon at the bottom-left corner of the graphics screen. This icon is used as a directional beacon while you work on your part. When you move the UCS, the icon will change to reflect the move. Even though you can turn the icon off, we recommend that you keep it visible so you don't get disoriented. Also, it should be set on the origin point.

Once you've identified the plane on which you'll be working, the UCS icon will reorient itself to help you identify the working surface. There are different forms of the UCS icon: the standard 2D wire version and the 3D wire version. Figure 2.4 shows the default sketch plane and the new sketch plane using the standard wire UCS icon. Look at the orientation of the icon in the figures. You can change which form of the UCS icon you want to display. This is explained in the next section. We prefer to use the 2D wire version because it makes it easier to see that the icon is flat against the surface you want to work on. We use this representation of the icon in most of the figures in this text.

UCS Icon Display

To control the display of the UCS icon, use the UCSICON command or the View/Display/UCS Icon pull-down menu item.

Figure 2.5(a) shows the standard 2D wire UCS icon. Note the W; when it's visible, the UCS and WCS are in alignment. When there's a cross (+) visible, it means that the icon is sitting directly on the UCS origin point (0,0,0).

Figure 2.5(b) shows the 3D wire UCS icon. With this form of the icon, the appearance of the box represents the alignment of the UCS with the WCS.

TIP: Moving Objects in 3D

When you want to move objects in three dimensions, you must know where the UCS is located so that you know which axis to move along. Initially the UCS is aligned with the WCS, so that the X and Y axes represent the horizontal plane, and the Z axis represents the elevation. Use the UCS icon to determine the location of the UCS.

Figure 2.4
(a) Default working plane; (b) new working plane and its effect on the UCS icon

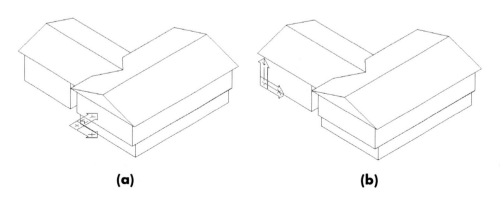

(a)   **(b)**

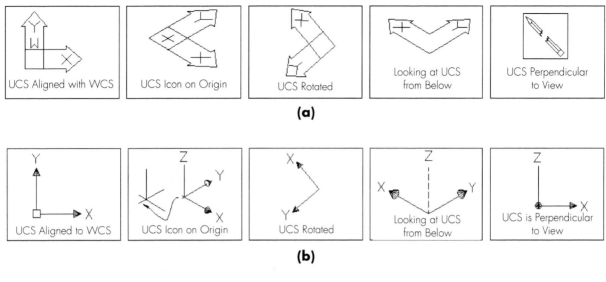

Figure 2.5   (a) 2D wire UCS icon, different orientations; (b) 3D wire UCS icon, different orientations; (c) UCS Icon dialog box

The following is a description of the options of the UCSICON command:

ON/OFF   The ON and OFF options either make the icon visible or cause it not to be displayed at all.

All   The All option applies changes to the icon in all active viewports. Otherwise, UCSICON affects only the current viewport.

Noorigin   The Noorigin option causes the icon to be displayed at the lower left of the graphics screen regardless of the actual location of the current UCS. A cross is not displayed in the center of the icon. This is sometimes useful when the icon is getting in the way of the geometry.

Origin   The Origin option causes the icon to be displayed on the 0,0,0 origin point of the current UCS. A cross is displayed on the icon to identify the origin point. However, if the icon cannot be fully displayed on the screen, such as when the origin point is panned off the display, the icon will revert to being displayed in the lower left of the screen until it can be fully displayed on the screen at the origin point. This does not mean that the origin point has changed, only the display of the UCS icon.

Properties   The Properties option controls the appearance of the 2D and 3D wire UCS icons. It will display a dialog box similar to Figure 2.5(c).

Shade Modes and the UCS Icon

Shade modes control how the design is displayed in a viewport. Normally, it is easier to display a wireframe for construction and use various forms of shading for visually examining the shape of the design. The common methods are wireframe and shaded, but there are currently seven methods in total. The View/Shade pull-down menu or the Shade toolbar will give you access to the various shade modes. The following tools are used to display different modes:

	2D Wireframe	Wireframe with 2D UCS icon
	3D Wireframe	Wireframe with 3D UCS icon
	Hidden	Hidden lines removed
	Flat Shade	Surfaces colored with flat tone
	Gouraud Shade	Surfaces colored with shades of color
	Flat Shade with edges	Flat shade with edges shown with lines
	Gouraud Shade with edges	Gouraud shade with edges shown with lines

 TIP: What Shade Mode Should Be Displayed?

As a beginner, you should work in wireframe mode. This makes it much easier to see the various edges, allowing you to pick them as needed. A 3D shade mode is useful when you want to check the object's current appearance. Switch back and forth as the design progresses.

Figure 2.6   UCS icon shown in 2D wireframe mode and 3D shade mode

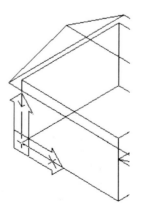 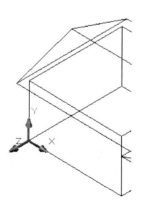

The shade mode option affects the display of the UCS icon. If the shade mode is set to 2D wireframe, the Wire icon is displayed; with any of the other shade modes the 3D Shaded icon is displayed. The 2D icon is more helpful in identification if the X and Y axes are flat or parallel with your object, whereas the 3D icon may make it easier to observe the Z axis. The choice is up to you. Figure 2.6 shows the icon in the two modes.

Viewing in 3D

When you physically hold an object in your hand, you're able to turn it around and view it from any angle. You can see the relationships each side or surface has with another. It helps you to understand the object better so that you are able to refine or alter it with more confidence.

The same principle applies when using Architectural Desktop; however, instead of moving the model, you move your viewing location. This is referred to as the *viewpoint*. You can think of it as if the model is suspended in midair, and you're able to walk around it, looking at it from above or below. As an added benefit, you're able to display multiple viewpoints of your design in separate viewports arranged in the graphics area. Some of the viewports can display your part as wireframe, while others can display it as a shaded view (see Figure 2.7). In this way you're able to see all around your model as you design it.

Think of it as if the model is suspended in midair, and you're able to walk around it, looking at it from above or below.

Preset Views

The fastest way to display different views of your model is to use the preset orthographic and isometric views. You can access the named views from a variety of sources. You can use the View/Named Views pull-down menu, or the View/3D Views pull-down menu,

Figure 2.7 Multiple viewports showing various viewpoints and shade modes

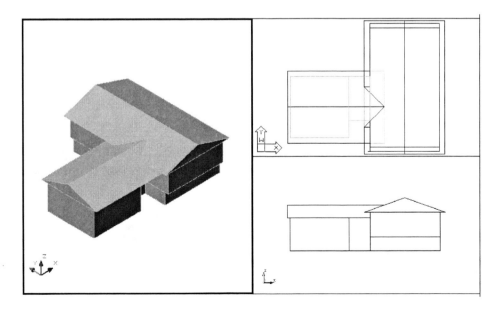

Figure 2.8   View
dialog box

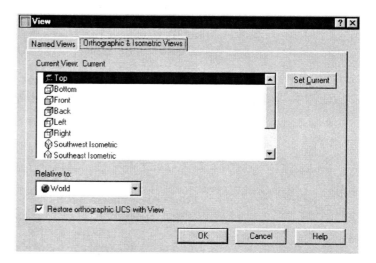

the View toolbar, or the Named Views flyout on the Standard toolbar at the top of the
screen. If you use the View/Named Views pull-down menu, a dialog box similar to Figure
2.8 appears. Refer to the dialog box to see the various orthographic and isometric views
such as Top and Southwest Isometric.

Whichever method you use, the picked view is displayed in the active viewport.
Using preset views, you can quickly switch viewpoints at any time.

3D Orbit

3DORBIT is a visually interactive method for displaying a view of the model. You can
access the command by typing it on the command line, picking it from the View pull-
down menu, or using the 3D Orbit tool.

When the command is activated, a large circle with four small circles appears on the
screen (see Figure 2.9). This is referred to as the *arc ball*. When you move your cursor
around, inside, or on the four small circles, the cursor changes to reflect the type of viewing rotation represented. Depending on where you pick and drag your cursor, the view
will rotate to a new position. Refer to Figure 2.9 and the following descriptions of the
rotation axes.

Circular   When you move the cursor outside the arc ball, the cursor changes to a
                   circular arrow. When you pick and drag around the outside of the arc ball,
                   the view rotation takes place around an axis that is perpendicular to the

Figure 2.9   Active
3DORBIT command
showing arc ball with
sample cursors added

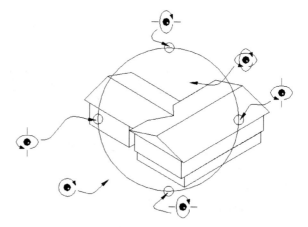

viewing plane or screen. When you release the pick button, the view rotation stops.

Horizontal   When you move the cursor into one of the small circles on the top or bottom side of the arc ball, the cursor changes to a horizontal elliptical arrow. When you pick and drag left or right, the view rotation takes place around a horizontal axis that is parallel to the viewing plane or screen. When you release the pick button, the view rotation stops.

Vertical   When you move the cursor into one of the small circles on the left or right of the arc ball, the cursor changes to a vertical elliptical arrow. When you pick and drag up or down, the view rotation takes place around a vertical axis that is parallel to the viewing plane or screen. When you release the pick button, the view rotation stops.

Spherical   When you move the cursor inside the arc ball, the cursor changes to a combination of the horizontal elliptical arrow and vertical elliptical arrow. When you pick and drag inside the arc ball, the view rotation takes place around both axes. When you release the pick button, the view rotation stops.

If you right-click while the 3DORBIT command is active, a context menu similar to Figure 2.10 appears.

Vpoint

A more precise way of setting the viewpoint is to use the VPOINT command. Using the command, you enter X, Y, and Z coordinates to place the viewer.

Positive X values place the viewer looking at the right side of the model. Negative X values place the viewer looking at the left side of the model.

Positive Y values place the viewer looking at the back side of the model. Negative Y values place the viewer looking at the front of the model.

Positive Z values place the viewer looking down at the top of the model. Negative Z values place the viewer below the model looking up at the bottom.

Figures 2.11 and 2.12 show different viewpoints with their X, Y, and Z coordinates.

Figure 2.10
3DORBIT shortcut menu

Figure 2.11
Viewpoints and their coordinates

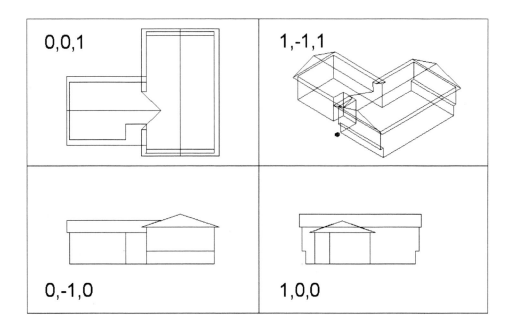

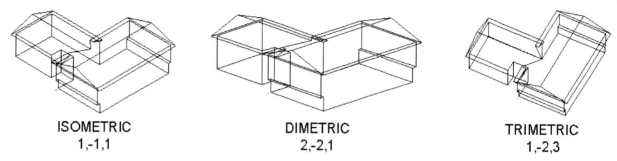

ISOMETRIC
1,-1,1

DIMETRIC
2,-2,1

TRIMETRIC
1,-2,3

Figure 2.12   Altering the view with different coordinate strengths

TIP: 3DORBIT versus VPOINT

Although the 3DORBIT command is very visual in the rotation of your view of the model, you can sometimes get disoriented in the movement of the view. The VPOINT command can give you more control in view placement. The VPOINT command is based on the WCS, and so its axes remain in the same orientation regardless of the view of the model. In this way you're always referring to the WCS, and you always have a concrete frame of reference.

A more precise way of setting the viewpoint is to use the VPOINT command.

You can access the command from the View/3D Views pull-down menu. You'll first be prompted to specify the viewpoint using the X, Y, and Z coordinates.

If you press Enter when asked for the coordinates, you're presented with a compass with which you can set the viewer location. Figure 2.13 shows the various parts of the compass axes labeled.

A nice feature of the VPOINT command is that it always performs a Zoom Extents to display your entire model when you enter the new viewpoint.

Saving and Restoring Views

Once you have a view that you think that you may want to apply from time to time, you can save the viewing position. To do this, use the VIEW command.

Figure 2.13   The input screen and the results

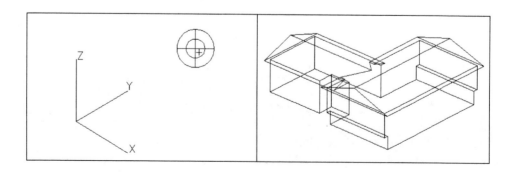

Select Named Views from the View pull-down menu. Using the View dialog box, you can create saved views by using the New button; to restore previously saved ones, highlight the name and pick the Set Current button.

Object Viewer

The Object Viewer is a separate window where you can view a selected object or several objects from your design. Use the Object Viewer to alter the viewpoint in order to examine the objects without changing the viewpoint in the viewports. If you like the view in the Object Viewer, you can apply it to the active viewport.

To use the Object Viewer, select one or more objects, right-click, and select Object Viewer from the context menu. A dialog box similar to Figure 2.14 appears.

Note the box containing the word SE Isometric on the far right of the viewer. Picking the down arrow displays a list of preset views, discussed earlier. *Note:* The preset views are based on the orientation of the current UCS.

Observe the four teapot-shaped tools at the top of the viewer. They display different shade modes. There are also tools for panning, zooming, and 3D orbit. To apply the current viewpoint contained in the viewer to the active viewport, pick the Set View tool.

The wide box displaying the word WORK contains a list of different display configurations that can be applied to the view. This was discussed in Chapter 1.

**Use the Object Viewer to alter the viewpoint
in order to examine the objects without
changing the viewpoint in the viewports.**

Figure 2.14 Object
Viewer window

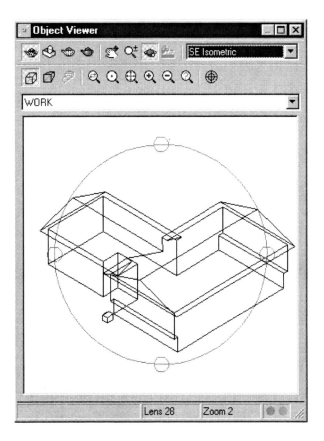

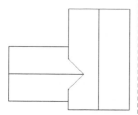

Figure 2.15   Simple design (plan view)

Hands-On: Viewing in 3D

This exercise provides practice in the use of the various methods of viewing a 3D model.

1. Open file ADTEX2A, which contains a simple design to which you'll apply different view methods. It should already be shown in Hidden Shade mode, as in Figure 2.15. If it is not, type SHADEMODE on the command line and enter Hidden.
    Make sure that the Model tab is active.

Using the View Presets

2. Pick and hold on the Named Views tool (at the top of the screen) to display the flyout. Slide down the flyout to the second tool, called Top View, and release the button. The Top view will be displayed. Now, go through the five other orthographic tools: Bottom, Left, Right, Front, Back. Observe the various orientations of the part. Watch the UCS icon to see which way the axes are pointing. Note that their orientation to the model never changes. Remember, the model is not moving. It is the viewer orientation that is moving.

3. Display a Front view and check that the Hidden Shade mode is turned on as described in Step 1.

4. Now, use the Named Views flyout and go through the four isometric views: Left front, Right front, Left back, and Right back. In each view, observe the orientation of the UCS icon.

Using 3D Orbit

5. Display a Top view of the design with Hidden Shade mode on. Zoom out 0.5×.

6. Pick the 3D Orbit tool. The arc ball appears overlaid on top of the part.
    Move your cursor around the arc ball. Pause on the inside and the outside and observe the shape of the cursor. Refer back to Figure 2.9. Identify the different cursor shapes. Move the cursor into each of the small circles and match the cursor shape to Figure 2.9.
    Move the cursor into the bottom small circle so that the cursor is displayed as the vertical elliptical arrow. Pick, hold, and drag the cursor upward and then downward but keep the pick button pressed. Note how the view of the part rotates. Display a view similar to Figure 2.16(a).
    Now pick in the right, small circle, hold, and drag left and right. Observe the rotation of the part. Display a view similar to Figure 2.16(b).
    Experiment with the other 3D Orbit cursor shapes to revolve the view.

Using Vpoint

7. Display a Wireframe Shade mode and use the SE Isometric view viewpoint tool to display an Isometric view.

Figure 2.16 Using the 3DORBIT command

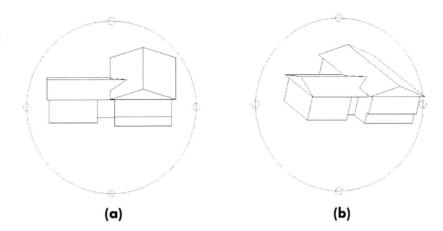

(a)   (b)

8.   Note how some of the roof lines overlap each other, making it hard to see all the lines. You are going to use the VPOINT command to remedy this by lowering and rotating the view.

Enter the VPOINT command and observe the coordinates. They should be $1,-1,1$. This is the viewpoint set by the tool you picked earlier. Now enter the value $1,-2,0.75$ and press Enter. Note how the view was lowered along the Z axis and turned more toward the Y axis.

9.   Enter the VPOINT command again and then press Enter to display the compass screen. Move the cursor around the circle compass and watch the orientation of the three axes. Remember that the front of the circle is the front of the model and that the small circle is above the model. Move the cursor into the small circle somewhere near the front and pick that location. What view did you get? Experiment with the compass to alter the view. As you can tell, this command is similar to the 3DORBIT command, except that the orientation is always based on the WCS. This keeps the model to always appear to sit flat. You may find that the 3DORBIT command is more visually reinforcing, but the VPOINT command can be more practical.

Object Viewer

10.   Now you're going to experiment with the Object Viewer. First, make sure that the grid is turned on. This helps with the orientation in the viewer.

Pick the model (it is all one object), and right-click to bring up the context menu. Select Object Viewer from the context menu. The Object Viewer window appears.

It is important that the display configuration drop-down list be set to WORK. This is the wide box just above the viewer's graphics area.

Using the viewer, display an SW Isometric view and turn Flat Shade mode on. Now, pick the Rendered Teapot tool and observe the different types of shading. They should be similar to Figure 2.17.

Experiment with the other tools to see their effects on the objects. As you can see, there are a variety of ways to view your model. You should be comfortable with moving around the model before you move on.

11.   Save your model as EX2A.

Figure 2.17 Object Viewer showing rendered shadows

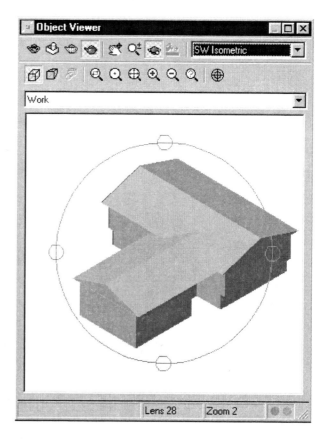

Working in 3D

Though most of your creation can take place on one plane, it is important to be able to work on other planes so that more complex creations are easier to organize and control. This is particularly important when working with the mass elements that will be discussed in the next chapter.

To create complex models, you have to be able to work on different planes and axes in 3D. As mentioned at the beginning of this chapter, all construction in 3D is still based on a flat (planar) 2D plane. In this section, you'll learn how to create this plane, which we refer to as the *working plane*.

Setting the UCS Working Plane

The UCS is an integral part of AutoCAD and was available to 3D modelers even before the creation of Architectural Desktop. Thus, you can move and reorient the UCS by various means. To set the UCS, type UCS on the command line. The following is a description of the UCS command's options:

UCS Option	Suboption	Description of Alignment or Option
New		
	Specify origin	Moves only the origin point; the alignment stays the same
	Zaxis	Defines the new direction of the positive Z axis

Figure 2.18 UCS and UCS II toolbars

	3Point	Defines the UCS by entering three points to define a plane; these points are origin, positive X-axis direction, and positive Y-axis direction
	OBject	Aligns the UCS with an existing object
	Face	Aligns the UCS with the face of a 3D solid
	View	Aligns the UCS with the plane of the current view
	X or Y or Z	Rotates the UCS about the selected axis
Move		
	Specify origin	Moves only the origin point; the alignment stays the same
	Zdepth	Moves the UCS along the Z axis
orthoGraphic		Aligns the UCS with preset planes such as Top and Front
Prev		Returns UCS alignment with the last UCS
Restore		Restores a saved UCS by name
Save		Saves the current UCS under a name
Del		Removes a named UCS
Apply		Applies the current UCS to a viewport

You can also set the UCS using the UCS and the standard ACAD UCS II toolbars, which are shown in Figure 2.18. The Tools pull-down menu contains various options for setting the UCS.

UCS and Viewports

The UCS can be set so that it is stored in the viewport. In this way, if you switch viewports, you can switch which working plane is active. For example, you could have the UCS set to match the WCS in the plan (top) view in one viewport and have the UCS match the front elevation in another viewport.

The UCS in each viewport is controlled by the UCSVP system variable. When UCSVP is set to 1 in a viewport, the UCS last used in that viewport is saved with the viewport and is restored when the viewport is made current again. When UCSVP is set to 0 in a viewport, its UCS is always the same as the UCS in the current viewport. Remember that the UCSVP system variable can be set to a different value in each viewport.

Architectural Desktop makes use of assigning UCSs to viewports. Thus, you should be aware that when you insert objects in one viewport they may have a different orientation if you insert them in another viewport, depending on the orientation of the UCS working plane.

TIP: UCS Icon Guide

Remember to turn on the UCS icon so that you can use it as a guide to determine where the UCS working plane is located. It is also useful to set the icon so that it is displayed on the origin point. This can help you determine the Z elevation of the working plane.

Hands-On: Moving the UCS Working Plane

In this exercise, you're going to move the UCS working plane around the model and create objects on different surfaces.

1. Open file ADTEX2B, which contains a simple model. Four viewports show the Top (plan), Front (elevation), Right side (elevation), and Isometric views. By default, the UCS working plane is set to the WCS. The UCSVP variable is set to 0. This causes only one UCS working plane to be shown in all viewports.

2. Make sure that the Model tab is active. Activate the Isometric viewport by picking inside the viewport.

UCS Icon Settings

3. The UCS icon should be visible and set to the origin. First, enter the UCS-ICON command and enter the All option, followed by the ON option. Repeat the UCSICON command, using the All option, followed by the Origin option. The All option is used to apply the next UCSICON command to every viewport.

UCS Working Plane Moved onto a Planar Surface

4. The first way of changing the UCS working plane is to align it with a surface (planar face) on the model. You're going to use the 3point option.

Make sure that the Endpoint running object snap is on. This makes it easier to select the points on the model.

Type UCS on the command line and proceed with the following prompts:

```
Command:                                 UCS
Current ucs name: *WORLD*
Enter an option [New/Move/orthoGraphic/
   Prev/Restore/Save/Del/Apply/?/World]
<World>:                                 New
Specify origin of new UCS or [ZAxis/3point/
   OBject/Face/View/X/Y/Z] <0,0,0>:      3
Specify new origin point <0,0,0>:        refer to the following text
```

At this point, the command is asking you where you want the new origin point to be located (see Figure 2.19). Pick point P1. Remember to use the object snap endpoint to lock the cursor at the correct location. The use of object snaps is extremely important when performing operations in 3D.

```
Specify point on positive portion of X-axis
   <1'-1 1/16",42'-3",0'-0">:            refer to the following text
```

Here, the program needs to know the direction in which you want the positive X axis to be pointing. An imaginary line is calculated from the new origin to the point. Pick for the positive direction of the X axis (see Figure 2.19). Pick point P2 (use object snap endpoint).

```
Specify point on positive-Y portion of the
UCS XY plane <1'-0 1/2",42'-3 15/16",0'-0">:  refer to the following text
```

This is where the program needs a point to calculate where the working plane is going to be. It pivots the plane around the new X axis based on the point picked for the positive Y (see Figure 2.19). Pick point P3 (use object snap endpoint).

Figure 2.19
Defining a new working
plane

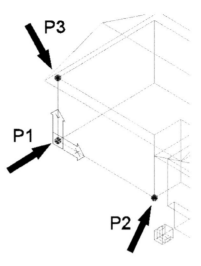

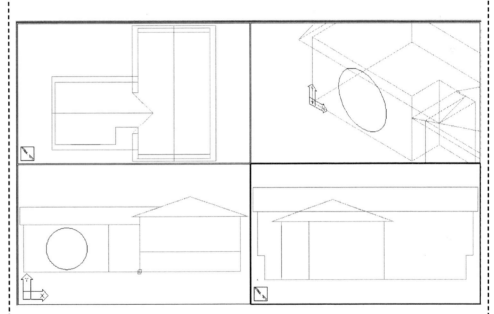

Figure 2.20   Drawing a circle on the wall

Note that the UCS icon has moved to indicate the new working plane. The icons in the Front and Isometric viewports are visible. Note how the icon in the Top and Side viewports is displayed as a broken pencil. This is to let you know that the UCS working plane is perpendicular to the viewport, and objects should not be drawn in those viewports using the current working plane. The UCS icon can be invaluable when performing 3D modeling on complex models.

5.   Activate the Front viewport. The UCS is aligned with that viewport.

6.   Draw a circle on the wall as shown in Figure 2.20.

7.   Repeat the steps to create UCS working planes on each of the walls, and draw a circle on each wall as you move the UCS. If you want the viewport to be parallel to the UCS working plane, enter the PLAN command and press Enter again to accept the default.

8.   Save your model as EX2B.

In a Nutshell

Being able to view your 3D model from various viewpoints is an important part of the design process. Using various tools, you can display isometric views in multiple viewports. Displaying the model in wireframe aids in construction, while shading the model can help with visual interpretation. The creation of UCS working planes is important in the creation and manipulation of objects.

   Now that you're comfortable moving around in 3D space, you're ready to start creating in Chapter 3.

 Testing... testing... 1, 2, 3

Fill-in-the-Blanks

1. You can access the preset named views of your model in four ways. They are:

    a._____

    b._____

    c._____

    d._____

2. List the seven shade modes. Put a check mark beside the two commonly used methods.

    _____   a._____

    _____   b._____

    _____   c._____

    _____   d._____

    _____   e._____

    _____   f._____

    _____   g._____

3. The _____ icon is used as a directional beacon while you work on your part. When you move the _____, the icon will _____ to reflect the move. Even though you can turn the icon _____, we recommend that you keep it _____ so you don't get disoriented.

True or False

4. A plane is defined by its XYZ coordinates.   T or F

5. You can set the UCS to match the WCS in the plan (top) view in one viewport, and you can set the UCS to match the front elevation in another viewport.   T or F

6. Working in 3D is easier than working in 2D.   T or F

7. Working in 3D allows speedier formulation of the design than working in 2D.
   T or F

8. The UCS is AutoCAD's master coordinate system.   T or F

Matching

9. Match the option or suboption of the UCS to its definition or function. You can use answers more than once.

(1)_____New-Specify origin
(2)_____New-Zaxis
(3)_____New-X or Y or Z
(4)_____Move-Specify origin
(5)_____Zdepth
(6)_____orthoGraphic
(7)_____Del

a. Aligns the UCS with preset planes such as Top and Front
b. Removes a named UCS
c. Moves the UCS along the Z axis
d. Rotates the UCS about the selected axis
e. Moves only the origin point; the alignment stays the same
f. Defines the new direction of the positive Z axis

What?

1. Explain the difference between the WCS and the UCS.
2. What is the right-hand rule?
3. What are the advantages and disadvantages of using 3DORBIT versus VPOINT?
4. Why is it important to be able to change your viewports?
5. Explain the purpose of having various shade modes.
6. What does the broken-pencil icon signify?
7. Describe the four areas of the 3D Orbit tool. Include their names, the appearance of their cursors, and their purposes.

Let's Get Busy!

1. Open file DESIGN2A, which contains a simple model with which you can practice visual manipulation.

   First, observe the location of the UCS by turning on the UCS icon and setting it to display on the origin point.

   Experiment with different shade modes by entering each viewport and displaying the model with different shade modes.

   Using the preset views, display a plan view, a front elevation, a side elevation, and an isometric view in each of the four viewports.

2. Open file DESIGN2B, which contains a simple model with which you can practice visual manipulation.

   Using 3D Orbit, practice manipulating the model so that you can view it from different viewpoints.

   Using the VPOINT command, practice the same type of manipulation until you are confident in displaying any viewpoint.

   Using the Object Viewer, practice manipulating the same model. Experiment with the different tools. When you have a view that you like, apply it to the different viewports.

3. Open file DESIGN2C, which contains a simple model with which you can practice creation of UCS working planes.

Create a UCS on the sloped roof of the building. Draw a rectangular box to represent a skylight.

Create a UCS on one of the front walls and draw a rectangle to represent a window and another to represent a door.

Set the UCS to match the WCS and move the small green box onto the small flat roof.

Chapter 3

Exterior Conceptual Design

Stonehenge

No matter what else it represents, Stonehenge has interesting architectural features, including this prominently displayed tenon on top of the standing stone on the right. The tenon would set into the mortice on the lintel that links two standing stones, such as the ones on the left. Although these stones currently date back three thousand to five thousand years, there was another stone circle on this site before this one was erected, and one made of wood predated that one!

Key Concepts

- ◆ Using Mass Elements
- ◆ Creating Mass Groups
- ◆ Using the Model Explorer
- ◆ Creating and Using Profiles

Conceptual Design

In conceptual design you assemble simple three-dimensional objects called *mass elements* to form the mass model that will represent the preliminary exterior design. You then attach these elements to form mass groups. During the attachment process, you can add, subtract, or intersect the various elements to create a complex building envelope (see Figure 3.1). At anytime during the conceptual phase you can resize the elements, and the mass model will change automatically to reflect the modification.

Once you have created the mass model, you can use it to start creating the building structure by slicing the model to create floorplates and by creating space boundaries for the preliminary design of the interior. This process will be discussed in the next chapter.

This chapter introduces you to mass modeling and the Model Explorer.

In conceptual design you assemble simple three-dimensional objects called mass elements to form the mass model that will represent the preliminary exterior design.

Mass Elements

A mass element is a parametric three-dimensional object. *Parametric* means that the shape of the object is controlled by a set of parameters. You can edit the object at any time and change its parametric properties. For example, the box mass element has three para-

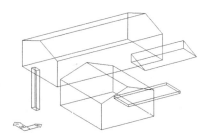 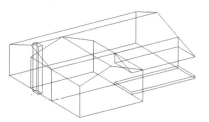 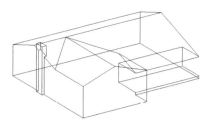

Figure 3.1   Mass elements grouped to form a mass model

Figure 3.2 Basic
mass elements

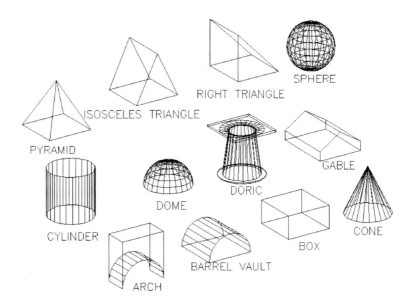

TIP: Creation Layer for Mass Elements

If you are using the AIA layer standards set by the Desktop/Drawing Setup, the
mass elements are created on the A-Mass layer and are colored magenta (purple).
The template file may set the color to gray. The iaadt3start.dwg maintains the
magenta color.

metric properties controlling its size and shape: length, width, and depth. By specifying
those parameters, you create the box. You can then modify those properties to change its
shape and size.

There are a series of basic shapes that you can use as building blocks. Figure 3.2
shows the various shapes from which you can choose. You can even create your own mass
element using a profile that you create. This feature is explained later in this chapter.

Adding Mass Elements

To create a mass element, use the Concept/Mass Elements/Add Mass Element pull-down
menu, or select the type of element from the Mass Elements toolbar, as shown in Figure
3.3. In either case, the Add Mass Element dialog box appears as shown in Figure 3.4.

Figure 3.3 Mass
Elements toolbar

Figure 3.4 Add
Mass Element dialog
box

TIP: Pushpin Button

A new feature has been added to some of the dialog boxes. If you look at the top-right corner of the Add Mass Element dialog box, you should notice a pushpin button next to the X button. When the pushpin button is pressed in, the dialog box's size is locked in place. When the pushpin button is not pressed in and you move your cursor off the dialog box, it will roll up, taking up less space. When you move the cursor over the dialog box, it will expand.

Once you have set the parameters in the Add Mass Element dialog box, leave the dialog box open and pick inside the viewport you want to create. You can then drag the mass element into the position you want. When dragging elements, you may see only a simplified version until the element is placed. Once have placed it, you can go back to the dialog box and start creating a new element. When you have finished placing elements, you can close the dialog box. When you want to create more elements, open the dialog box, set the parameters, and place the new element.

The following describe various areas contained within the dialog box.

Shape   The Shape drop-down list is used to choose the shape of the element to add.

Profile   The Profile drop-down list is used to select profiles to create more complex elements. There are preconfigured profiles from which to choose. You can also create your own, as explained at the end of this chapter.

Size Boxes   The other text boxes are used to control the size of the mass element. The types of boxes presented change depending on the type of element to be created.

Tools   There are several tools that are used to aid in construction. The first tool, called the Floating Viewer, is used to display a window that allows you to view the element before you place it. This can be useful when you have a complex element. The viewer is similar to the Object Viewer discussed in Chapter 2.

There are also tools for matching properties to an existing element and for modifying properties of the current element.

Placing Mass Elements

When first creating your mass elements, you can either place them accurately while creating each one or place them randomly and then assemble them into relative positions. In either case, the key to remember is that they are three-dimensional objects and as such must relate to one another in a three-dimensional way. This is the reason that we reviewed 3D concepts in Chapter 2 before moving onto creation.

Just like building blocks, the mass elements can be placed beside one another or stacked on top of one another. This placement involves movement in three dimensions. It is easy to place objects while looking at a plan view using the X and Y axes, but to place them on top of one another requires elevation views and isometric views as well as movement in the Z axis. Figure 3.5 shows a plan view and an isometric view of some placed mass elements.

The Mass-Group tab at the bottom of the graphics screen is used to place mass elements and then group them together. The different display systems applied to each viewport allow mass elements to be seen in one viewport and mass groups to be seen in another. This feature will be useful when you get to the grouping stage, but while you are starting to assemble mass elements it is sometimes more practical to change the display system applied to the group viewport so that it displays mass objects.

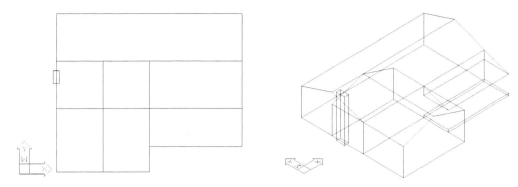

Figure 3.5   Two viewports showing plan and isometric views

> ### TIP: Placing Mass Elements
> ###   with Object Snaps
>
> One way to simplify placement is to use object snaps. You can snap onto objects in a three-dimensional way just the same as you did in two dimensions. In this way if you first place elements on ground level, you can use object snaps to place other elements on top of them.

When first creating your mass elements you can either place them accurately while creating each one or place them randomly and then assemble them into relative positions.

In this way you'll have two viewports to display different views of your mass elements as you create and assemble them. You'll get hands-on practice doing this in the next exercise.

Hands-On: Using Mass Elements

This is an initial training exercise in which you'll create some mass elements and manipulate them to create a basic design. Later on in this chapter you'll use these elements to create a mass group. At the end of the chapter you'll practice what you have learned on the bank model.

1.   Open file IAADT3START, which is the startup file on the CD-ROM with this text. It contains the necessary startup settings. Save this drawing as EX3A.

2.   Display the View toolbar and dock it at the right of the screen. You'll be switching to different views often in your design. You should make it a habit to display the View toolbar.

3.   Open the Desktop pull-down menu and pick the Drawing Setup item. Review the dialog boxes without changing anything. This will let you see what has already been set for you. When you're finished with your review, pick the Cancel button to close the dialog box.

4.   Open the Mass Elements toolbar and drag it into the upper-right corner of the graphics screen without docking it.

5.   Pick the Mass-Group layout tab at the bottom of the graphics screen.

6.   Activate the left viewport and set it to display the top (plan) view. Use the Top view tool in the View toolbar. Use Zoom All to zoom to the limits.

7.   Activate the right viewport. It is normally used to display and work with mass groups. For now, you're going to change its display system so that it displays mass elements.

Open the Desktop pull-down menu and pick Select Display from the menu. The Viewport Display Configuration dialog box appears. Note how the Concept_Group name is highlighted. That is the display system currently applied to the viewport. Highlight Concept_Mass and pick OK. This applies the Concept_Mass display system to the viewport.

8.   With the right viewport still active, pick the SE Isometric view tool and Zoom All.

Adding Mass Elements

9.   Move your cursor slowly over the various tools on the Mass Elements toolbar, pausing at each one so that you can see the tooltip. There are 11 basic shapes. There are more complex elements, but they do not have tools.

10.   Pick the Box tool from the Mass Elements toolbar. When the Add Mass Element dialog box appears, drag it to the upper part of the graphics screen. Set the width to 40′, the depth to 20′, and the height to 10′. Pick in the right viewport and then place the center of the box at 50′,30,0′ and press Enter to accept the rotation of 0. Your screen should look similar to Figure 3.6. Leave the Add Mass Element dialog box open.

11.   Open the Shape drop-down list in the Add Mass Element dialog box and select Right Triangle from the list. Set the width to 40′, the depth to 20′, and the height to 10′. Pick in the right viewport and place the wedge shape anywhere. Press Enter to accept the rotation of 0. Close the dialog box.

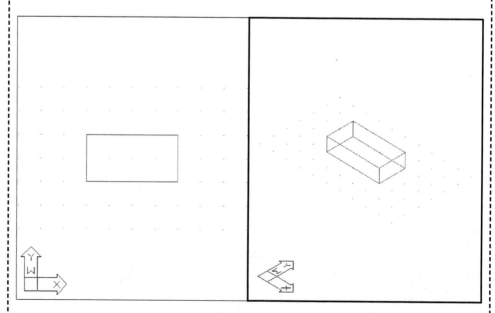

Figure 3.6   Adding the box mass element

Figure 3.7 Wedge
placed on top of box

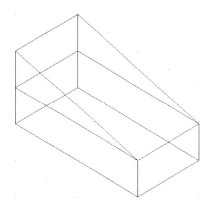

12.   Use the MOVE command to move the wedge on top of the box. Use End-point object snap, and use the bottom corner of the wedge as the base point, and the top corner of the box as the destination. The results should look like Figure 3.7.

Modifying Mass Elements

You're going to change the size of the box and wedge by modifying their properties.

13.   With no command active, pick the box to highlight it. Right-click to bring up the context menu. Pick Properties from the list. The Mass Element Properties dialog box appears. Pick the Dimensions tab. Change the depth to 30', and OK the dialog box. The depth of the box should have enlarged to 30'.

Repeat the procedure with the wedge to increase its depth to 30'.

Adding More Elements

14.   Pick the Cylinder tool from the Mass Elements toolbar. Enter a 30' height and a 6' radius. Place the cylinder at 30',30',0' and press Enter to accept a rotation of 0. Close the Add Mass Element dialog box.

15.   You're now going to create a UCS working plane on the slope of the wedge.

Activate the right viewport and enter the UCSICON command. Enter the ORigin option to display the icon on the origin point.

Create the UCS working plane by referring to Figure 3.8 and proceed with the following:

Command:	**UCS**
Current ucs name: *WORLD*	
Enter an option [New/Move/orthoGraphic/ Prev/Restore/Save/Del/Apply/?/World] <World>:	**New**
Specify origin of new UCS or [ZAxis/3point/ OBject/Face/View/X/Y/Z] <0,0,0>:	**3**
Specify new origin point <0,0,0>:	**Using Endpoint object snap, snap to P1**.
Specify point on positive portion of X-axis <1'-1 1/16",42'-3",0'-0">:	**Using Endpoint object snap, snap to P2**.

Specify point on positive-Y portion of the UCS
    XY plane <1'-0 1/2",42'-3 15/16",0'-0">:
	**Using Endpoint object snap, snap
	    to P3**.

The UCS icon should now be on the corner of the sloped surface.

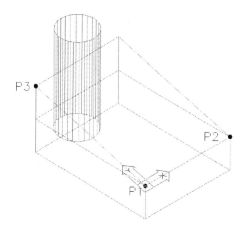

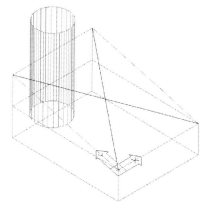

Figure 3.8   Creating a UCS working plane on the sloped surface

Figure 3.9   Crossing lines on sloped surface

16.   Using the LINE command, draw two lines that cross each other from corner to corner of the sloped surface (see Figure 3.9). These will be used to determine an intersection point in the next step.

17.   Activate the left viewport, display a front view, and then reactivate the right viewport.

18.   Now you're going to create a pyramid shape on the slope. From the Mass Elements toolbar, select the Pyramid tool. Enter a width of 20′, a depth of 20′, and a height of 5′. Pick in the right viewport and snap on the intersection of the two lines to place the pyramid mass element. Enter 45 for the rotation angle. The pyramid should now appear on the sloped surface as shown in Figure 3.10.

It is extremely important to remember which viewport is active when placing objects. Whichever UCS is set in the viewport determines the orientation of

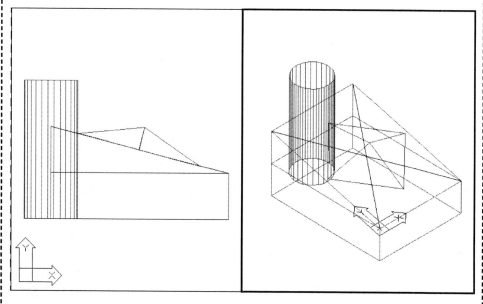

Figure 3.10   Pyramid added to sloped surface

the object. The right viewport is set to the slope, while the left viewport is set to the side.

19.   Erase the crossing lines and save your drawing as EX3A.

Mass Groups

Once you've created your mass elements, the next step is to combine them into mass groups to create complex shapes. You can add and subtract elements from one another to create the resulting intersecting masses. The group information is stored in a new object called a *mass group marker*. It is a three-dimensional symbol of a series of boxes that contains all the grouping information. Whenever you want to modify the group, you need to refer to the 3D symbol for that group. Figure 3.11 shows several mass elements, the resulting mass group, and the 3D mass group marker.

You can use the Concept/Mass Groups pull-down menu or the Mass Groups toolbar, shown in Figure 3.12.

TIP: Creation Layer for Mass Groups

If you are using the AIA layer standards set by the Desktop/Drawing Setup, the mass groups are created on the A-Mass-Grps layer and are colored cyan (light blue). The template file may set the color to khaki. The iaadt3start.dwg maintains the cyan color.

Figure 3.11   (a) Mass elements; (b) mass group with mass group marker

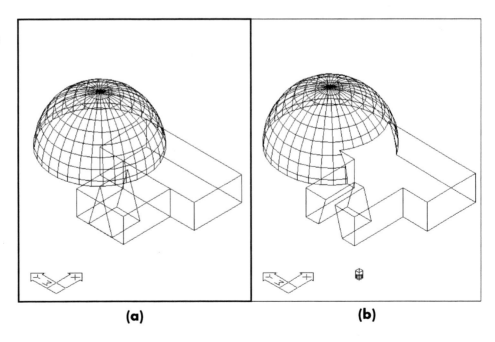

(a)   (b)

Figure 3.12   Mass Groups toolbar

TIP: Mass Group Marker Display

You may find that the group mass marker disappears from the screen for no apparent reason. There are some factors that govern its display. The symbol is only visible in 2D wireframe shade mode. If you use any other shade or hide mode, the marker will not show. Also, the marker changes size depending on your zoom factor. If you zoom out, the marker may disappear. Regenerate the viewport; the marker will resize itself to a small box shape.

Adding the Mass Group Marker

The first step in creating a mass group is to create the mass group marker. Either pick the Add Mass Group tool, or select Add Mass Group from the Concept/Mass Groups pull-down menu. You'll be prompted to indicate where you want to locate the mass group marker. The location itself is not important, but you must be able to locate the marker when you want to modify the mass group. Usually it is placed near the WCS 0,0,0. If you have more than one mass group, you'll need to situate each marker at a different location.

Mass Group Properties

The mass group marker contains all the properties of the group. You can access these properties by highlighting the marker or group and right-clicking to bring up the context menu. From the menu, select Grouping Properties. You can use this option to describe the group for later reference.

Attaching Elements to the Group

To combine the elements, you need to attach the various mass elements to the mass group. To do this, pick the Attach Elements tool, or select Attach Elements from the Concept/Mass Groups pull-down menu. You'll be prompted to select the mass group that you created previously. This is where you must pick the mass group marker. Once you have picked the marker, you can pick as many elements as you want to attach, pressing Enter to complete the attachment.

You can also detach an element from a group at any time.

Boolean Operations

When you attach an element to a group, you have three choices for the type of attachment: add, subtract, or intersect. These are referred to as *Boolean operations*. By default, the element is added to the group. If you right-click on the mass element and pick Element Properties from the context menu, a dialog box appears. Under the Mass Group tab you can change the operation from add to subtract or intersect. The attachment changes the relationship of the element to the group to which it belongs.

TIP: Display of Mass Elements and Groups

The display of mass elements and groups is controlled by the display system applied to the viewport. If you do not see a certain object type in a viewport, you may need to apply a display system to the viewport.

Figure 3.13 Model
Explorer dialog box

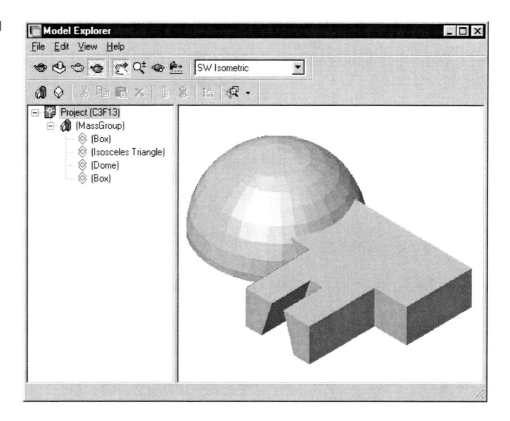

When you attach an element to a group, you have three
choices for the type of attachment: add, subtract, or
intersect. These are referred to as Boolean operations.

Model Explorer

The Model Explorer is a window in which you can create, view, and manipulate mass elements and mass groups (see Figure 3.13). As you can see, it looks similar to the Object Viewer. It operates in the same way as the Object Viewer except that it displays only mass elements and mass groups.

The main difference between the two dialog boxes is the addition of the group/element hierarchy tree list at the left in the Model Explorer screen. This tree lists the groups and elements contained in any drawings that you have open. Using the tree, you can drag elements from one group to another.

Above the graphics area of the dialog box is a set of tools that you can use to manipulate groups. You can create new groups or elements, and attach or detach elements, as well as cut and paste.

Some people prefer to use the Model Explorer to perform all their mass modeling.

Hands-On: Creating Mass Groups

The purpose of this exercise is to give you practice creating and manipulating mass groups. You will make use of the mass elements you created in the last Hands-On.

1.   Open file EX3A, which you created previously.

2.   Open the Mass Groups toolbar and drag it into the upper-right corner of the graphics screen without docking it.

3.   Pick the Mass-Group layout tab at the bottom of the graphics screen.

4.   Activate the right viewport. In the last exercise, you changed the display system to display mass elements. To work with mass groups, the display system has to be changed back.

Open the Desktop pull-down menu and pick Select Display from the menu. The Viewport Display Configuration dialog box appears. Note how the Concept_Mass name is highlighted. That is the display system currently applied to the viewport. Highlight Concept_Group and pick OK. This applies the Concept_Group display system to the viewport. The elements in the right viewport should disappear. Only groups are now visible in that viewport.

5.   Using the View tools, display an SE Isometric view in both viewports.

6.   Set the UCS to World in both viewports.

```
Command:                              UCS
Current ucs name: *WORLD*
Enter an option [New/Move/orthoGraphic/
    Prev/Restore/Save/Del/Apply/?/World]
<World>:                              World
```

Adding the Mass Group Marker

7.   Activate the right viewport and pick the Add Mass Group tool from the Mass Tools toolbar. Enter 30′,10′,0′ for the location. The group mass marker is probably not visible on your screen. Use the ZOOM EXTENTS command to display it. You may need to use the REGEN command to regenerate the geometry to see the group marker. Then use Zoom Window to get a closer look. It is a cyan-colored 3D symbol composed of interlocking boxes.

Attaching Elements

8.   The order in which the elements are selected controls their order in the mass group. For this step, select the cylinder last.

Select the Attach Elements tool from the Mass Groups toolbar. You will be asked to select the mass group. Pick the mass group marker and select all the elements in the left viewport. Press Enter to complete the process.

Normally, the group would now appear in the right viewport, but you may have zoomed in too close to see it. Use the ZOOM EXTENTS command to display it. Compare the mass group on the right in Figure 3.14 with the mass elements on the left. The group is one integral object. Note that the lines representing individual elements are gone. Enter the REGEN command to make the mass group marker appear.

Model Explorer

9.   Open the Concept pull-down menu and select Show Model Explorer. A Model Explorer window similar to Figure 3.15 should appear.

The View Control drop-down list probably is showing the Top view. Pick it and change it to an SE Isometric view.

Move through the four different shade modes, picking each one in turn. Observe the effect of each on the view.

Highlight the name [Mass Group] located in the tree list and right-click it. From the context menu, select Grouping Properties. This will display a dialog box similar to Figure 3.16. In the description box, enter My First Group and then

Figure 3.14   (a)
Mass elements and (b)
mass group

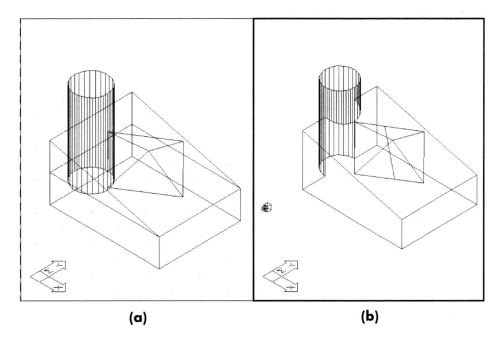

(a)   **(b)**

pick OK. Observe the tree now. The name My First Group has been added. It is
important to name the objects in your model to help keep track of them.

   Pick on the plus (+) sign next to the My First Group name to open up the
tree. As you can see, all the elements in the group are listed. Add names to each
of the elements in the same way you did for the group: highlight, right-click
Element Properties, and enter a description under the General tab. Use the following names: Box is called BASE, Right Triangle is called ROOF, Pyramid is
called SKYLIGHT, and Cylinder is called COLUMN. Did you notice that
when you highlighted the element it was displayed in the window?

Figure 3.15   Model
Explorer dialog box

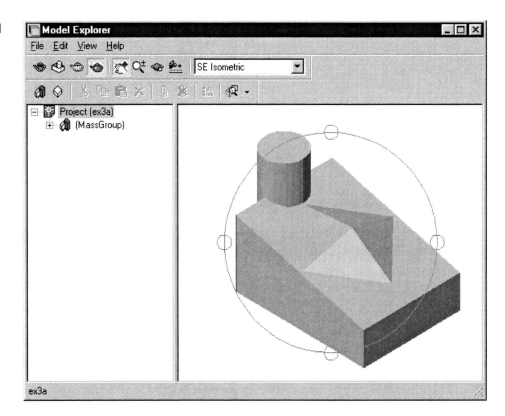

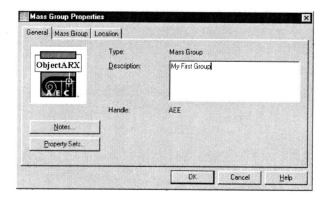

Figure 3.16   Mass Group Properties dialog box

You're now going to change the Boolean operation of the column. Highlight its name and right-click. From the context menu, pick Element Properties. When the Mass Element Properties dialog box appears, pick the Mass Group tab. Change the add operation to subtract and pick OK to exit.

Highlight My First Group in the tree and observe the window. The column has now been subtracted from the group to form a semicircular cutout.

Display an SW Isometric view. Modify the column's element properties again. This time, under dimensions, change the radius to 12′ and OK to exit. Highlight My First Group again. See the results. The column has cut through every element. You can make changes to an element at any time, and its alteration will be reflected in the group. Figure 3.17 shows the results of the radius change.

10.   Close the Model Explorer window to see the changes in your model.

11.   Save your file as EX3B.

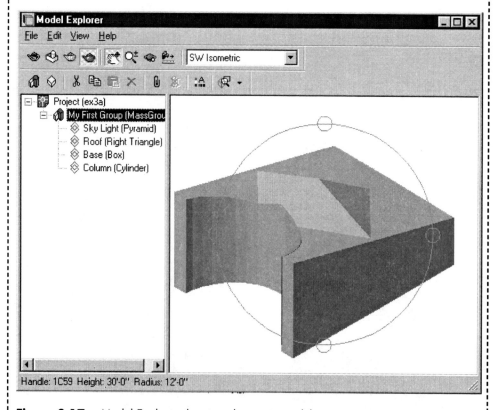

Figure 3.17   Model Explorer showing change in model

Profiles

Profiles are used to create more complex shapes by taking a 2D polyline and extruding or revolving it into a three-dimensional shape. You can use profiles to create complex mass elements, but you can also use them to create custom objects such as convoluted wall openings.

Creating a Profile from a Polyline

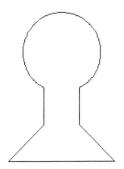

Figure 3.18   2D closed polyline

To create a profile, you must first draw a closed 2D polyline. If you desire, you can include interior 2D polyline islands as long as they don't cross each other (see Figure 3.18).

Once you have the polyline, open the Desktop pull-down menu, and select Profiles/ Profile Definitions. You are presented with a dialog box similar to Figure 3.19. The list contains all the standard profiles that come with Architectural Desktop and any profiles that you choose to add.

To import styles, all you need to do is select the Style Manager's File/Open pull-down menu. You can pick the drawing to open in the Style Manager. All the styles located in the opened drawing will be displayed. Figure 3.19 shows an open Drawing3 that has the typical startup styles and open drawing Profiles (Imperial). The Profiles drawing file contains more profile types. To use one of the styles, simply pick from one list and drag to the other. Note the path of the profile styles. Pausing your cursor over an open drawing displays its path name.

To create a new profile, pick the New Style button, and you'll be asked to name the profile. It is then added to the list. Highlight the name in the list, right-click, and then pick the Set From button in the context menu. You'll then be asked to pick the 2D polyline from the drawing. Next, you'll be asked if you want to add another ring. This is where you can add island polylines to the overall shape. Answer No if you have just one

Figure 3.19   Profiles dialog box used to create a new profile

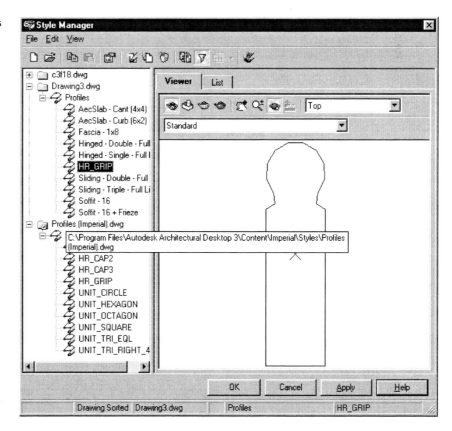

polyline. You are then asked for the insertion point. You can pick a point or press Enter to use the centroid. The profile is then defined by the 2D closed polyline.

You can copy, edit, import, or export profiles.

You can also insert a profile as a polyline into a drawing by using the Desktop/Profiles/Insert Profile as Polyline pull-down menu item. You can then modify the polyline and save it as a new profile.

Using a Profile as an Element

To use a profile as a mass element, open the Add Mass Element dialog box, and from the Shape list select either Extrusion or Revolution. The former extrudes the profile shape along the Z axis, whereas the latter revolves the profile shape around the Z axis about the center of the profile.

Once you have picked either Revolution or Extrusion, you then have access to the Profile list. From the list you can select your profile and then specify the size properties to create the three-dimensional mass element. Figure 3.20 shows the dialog box and the profile mass element on the drawing.

In a Nutshell

Conceptual design involves the use of mass elements, which are forms of basic building blocks, to create an exterior mass model. You can combine them to create mass groups to form complex shapes. You can attach elements to groups either by addition, subtraction, or intersection. To further add to the complexity of mass elements, you can create profiles from 2D polylines that can be extruded or revolved to form three-dimensional shapes.

To aid in the creation of 3D mass models, you have access to the Model Explorer. The Model Explorer contains all the commands necessary to create elements and groups as well as other tools such as the hierarchy tree list.

Now that you have seen how to create a conceptual design of the exterior, the next chapter will give you insight into the design of interior spaces.

Figure 3.20   Add Mass Element dialog box showing extruded profile

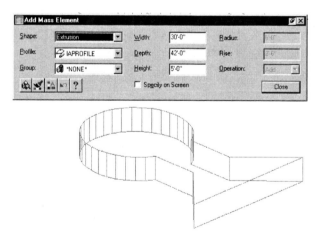

Testing... testing... 1, 2, 3

Fill-in-the-Blanks

1. The Add Mass Element dialog box contains four general areas:

   a._____

   b._____

   c._____

   d._____

2. You can perform many operations on a profile. You can:

   a._____

   b._____

   c._____

   d._____

3. When you add mass elements, they are placed on the _____. This placement is controlled by the _____ set by the Desktop/Drawing Setup.

4. The group information is stored in a new object called a(n) _____. It is a(n) _____ symbol that contains all the grouping information.

5. The first step in creating a mass group is to create the _____ . Usually it is placed near the _____ .

6. The three possible Boolean operations are:

   a._____

   b._____

   c._____

True or False

7. The initial location of the mass group marker is not important.   T or F

8. Profiles can be used to extrude or revolve a 2D polyline into a three-dimensional shape.   T or F

9. The mass elements can't be placed beside one another but can be stacked on top of one another.   T or F

10. Mass elements are attached to form mass groups.   T or F

What?

1. Explain the difficulty with stacking mass elements in three dimensions.

2. What is the Model Explorer and what are its functions?

3. How do you access Mass Group Properties?

4. Outline the procedure for adding a mass element.

5. "When first creating your mass elements, you can either place them accurately while creating each one, or place them randomly and then assemble them into relative positions." What would be the advantages and disadvantages of these two methods?

6. What is the Floating Viewer?

Let's Get Busy!

1. Create the mass elements shown in Figure 3.21(a). Create a mass group called Temple, and attach the elements to form the mass model shown in Figure 3.21(b). You will need to use different Boolean operations to form the final group.

2. Create the mass elements shown in Figure 3.22(a). Figure 3.22(c) shows the front elevation view. Create a mass group called Bungalow and attach the elements to form the mass model shown in Figure 3.22(b).

3. Create the mass elements shown in Figure 3.23(a). Create a mass group called Office and attach the elements to form the mass model shown in Figure 3.23(b). You will need to use different Boolean operations to form the final group. Figure 3.23(c) shows the plan view.

Figure 3.21   Ancient temple

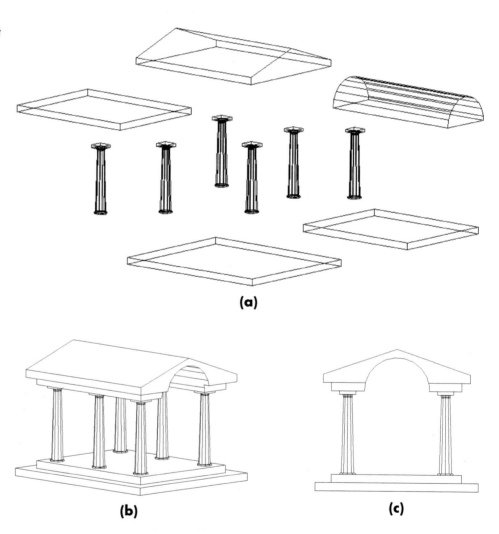

(a)

(b)   (c)

Figure 3.22
Bungalow

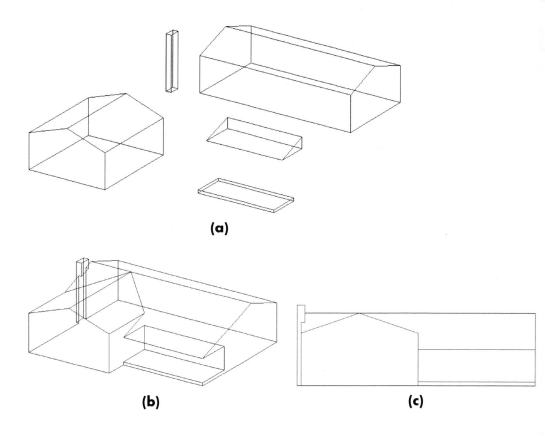

(a)

(b)   **(c)**

Figure 3.23 Office
building complex

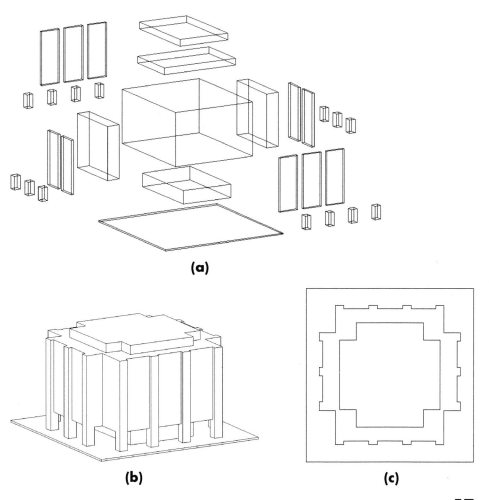

(a)

(b)   **(c)**

Chapter 4
Spatial Planning

Urkhart Castle on Loch Ness

By examining ruins of past structures, architects obtain many clues about the building of their predecessors. Look closely at this photo and you might even spot the Loch Ness Monster.

Key Concepts

◆ Floorplates
◆ Space Planning
◆ Space Boundaries

Spatial Planning

There are several ways to approach spatial planning within Architectural Desktop. The first way is to make use of the mass model by slicing it into floorplates that represent the exterior profile of the model. Another way is to use interior spaces and assemble them into an over-all interior layout. A third option is to combine these two approaches at any time as the necessity arises. A final choice is to apply space boundaries that are used as dividers between spaces. These boundaries can eventually be turned into walls where applicable.

Floorplates

Once you have created the mass model, you can slice the model horizontally to create perimeter profiles. These profiles are referred to as *floorplates*. The floorplates are linked to the mass group. If you change any element in the group, the floorplate changes as well. You can create slices at various elevations to create different floorplates. These floorplates can then be used to create space boundaries that, in turn, can be used to create walls. Figure 4.1(a) shows floorplates; Figure 4.1(b) shows the Slice Floorplates toolbar.

Figure 4.1
(a) Floorplates; (b) Slice Floorplates toolbar

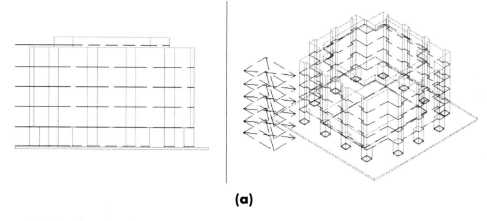

(a)

(b)

Slice Marker

To create a floorplate, you first need to create a slice marker. This marker determines the elevation of the slice and the objects to be included in the slice. To create a slice marker, select the Generate Slice tool from the Slice Floorplates toolbar, or open the Concept pull-down menu and select Slice Floorplates/Generate Slice.

You'll be asked first for the number of slices to create and then to specify the lower-left and upper-right corners for the slice marker. The actual size of the marker is important only in the sense that you must be able to see it. Its properties extend to infinity along the elevation on which it is created. As with the mass group marker, you'll be asked for the location and rotation. If you create only one slice at a time, you'll be asked for a starting height for its elevation. If, however, you create more than one, you'll be asked for the starting height and the distance between slices. The marker appears as a rectangle with an X through it.

Slice Elevation

You can change the elevation of a slice at any time by highlighting the slice and right-clicking to bring up the context menu. From the menu, select Set Elevation. You can also use the Concept/Slice Floorplates/Set Slice Elevation pull-down menu item or use the Set Elevation Tool from the Slice Floorplates toolbar.

When you change the elevation of the slice, the represented floorplate changes to reflect the new elevation. You won't see a floorplate until you attach a group to the slice marker.

The slice marker determines the elevation of the slice and the objects to be included in the slice.

Attaching Objects

Once the slice has been created, you need to attach mass elements or a mass group to the slice marker. You can use the context menu or select the Concept/Slice Floorplates/

Figure 4.2 Slice and attached group showing dashed line representing the floorplate

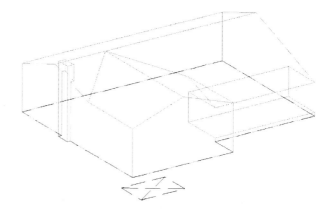

Attach Objects pull-down menu item or use the Set Elevation Tool from the Slice Floorplates toolbar. You're first asked to select the slice and then to identify the elements. It's usually better to select the mass group so that the Boolean operations can be applied as well. Figure 4.2 shows the marker with the attached group. Note the dashed line representing the floorplate perimeter of the model at the slice elevation.

You can detach objects from the slice or attach more at any time.

Slice Properties

Like any other object in Architectural Desktop, the slice object has properties. You can change its location and give it a name. It is a good idea to give a slice a name so that you can identify it more easily. If you zoom in close on the slice marker, you'll see a text object with the elevation of the slice (see Figure 4.3). To access a slice's properties, highlight it, right-click, and select Slice Properties from the context menu.

Converting to a Polyline

From the floorplate, you can create a closed polyline. The polyline can be used to create spaces or walls. It's important to note that once the polyline is created, it has no link to the floorplate. If you want the polyline to reflect a change in the floorplate, you'll have to erase the old polyline and create a new one. To create a polyline, use the Convert to Polyline tool or open the Concept pull-down menu and select Slice Floorplates/Convert to Polyline. Figure 4.4 shows the results of the converted polyline.

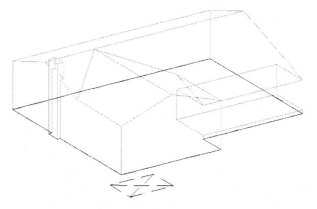

Figure 4.3 Slice marker showing elevation text

Figure 4.4 Polyline generated from floorplate

TIP: Polyline from Slice

The polyline that is created from a floorplate slice is an object on its own and is created on the current layer. A good idea is to create a layer for the polyline before you create it. This will help you keep your design organized.

Hands-On: Creating Floorplates

In this exercise you'll create a floorplate by creating a slice marker and then attaching a group to the marker. You'll use the floorplates to create polyline profiles.

1.   Open file ADTEX4A. It contains a mass model of an office complex that you'll slice into floorplates.

2.   Make sure the Slice Floorplates toolbar is visible and that you have activated the Mass-Group tab. Check to make sure the LTSCALE is set to 200. This will allow you to see the dashed lines that represent the floorplates when they're created.

Generating Slices

3.   Activate the right viewport and select the Generate Slice tool from the Slice Floorplates toolbar. Proceed with the following prompts:

Number of slices <1>:	**3**
First corner:	**0,0**
Second Corner or [Width]:	**20',20'**
Rotation <0.00>:	**0**
Starting height <0">:	**0**
Distance between slices <1'-0">:	**30'**

Three slices are created, the first starting at an elevation of 0, and the next two continuing at 30-ft intervals. Figure 4.5 shows the newly generated slices.

Figure 4.5   Three newly created slices

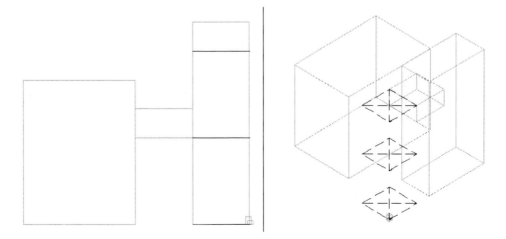

Figure 4.6 Attached objects creating the floorplates

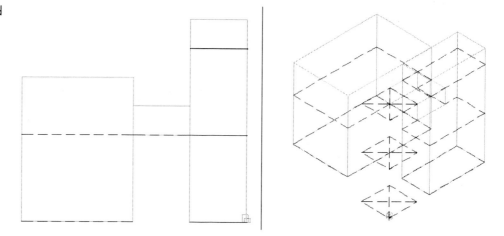

Attaching the Group

4.   The next step is to attach a group to the slice to create the floorplate. Select the Attach Objects tool. You'll be asked to select the slices. Select all three slices and press Enter. You'll then be asked to select the elements. In this case, select the cyan-colored mass-group marker in the right viewport and press Enter. The three floorplates are then created as shown in Figure 4.6.

Refer to the left viewport showing a side elevation view. You should be able to see the red lines representing the three floorplates. Note their locations. Each floorplate has a different profile depending on where it cuts through the mass model group.

Creating a Polyline

5.   You're now going to create a polyline profile of each floorplate so that you can see different profile shapes. Select the Convert to Polyline tool. You'll be asked to select slices. Select the bottommost slice only and press Enter. Two polyline profiles are then created. To see the polylines, switch to the Space layout, as shown in Figure 4.7. There are two profiles because of the slice elevation.

6.   Erase the two polylines and switch back to the Mass-Group layout.

7.   Repeat the Convert to Polyline sequence. This time select the second slice marker. Switch to the Space layout and observe the shape of the profile.

Figure 4.7 Space layout showing polyline profiles

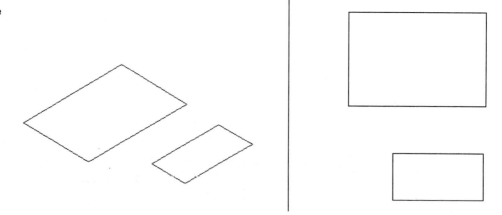

8. Repeat Steps 6 and 7. This time select the top slice marker. Note how the profiles all changed depending on their elevation.

Remember that you can change the elevation (using the Set Slice Elevation command) of a slice at anytime, and the floorplate will change to reflect the new elevation; however, the polyline will not change. You must erase it and generate a new one.

9. Save your file as EX4A.

Space Planning

There are two approaches to space planning. You can work with the exterior envelope of the building and fit spaces into it, or you can define spaces and assemble them, thus creating the exterior shape and size. The Spaces toolbar accesses most of the spacing planning commands. Figure 4.8 shows the toolbar.

It is important to note that once you move into space planning there is no direct link back to the mass model. Each plan that you create at this point is completely independent of the exterior mass model. Consequently, you can add and modify the plan to suit the next stage of development without the added restrictions of the initial mass model. The final link between the mass model and space planning is the polyline exterior profile created from a floorplate.

When spaces are created, they appear as brown-colored rectangles that are filled with brown cross-hatching.

In space planning you can work with the exterior envelope of the building and fit spaces into it, or you can define spaces and assemble them, thus creating the exterior shape and size.

Using the Polyline Exterior Profile: Outside-In

The first approach to space planning makes use of the mass model. Once you have created a polyline slice of the mass model, you can convert it into a space or simply use it as a controlling envelope within which to fit your spaces. The creation of the slice polyline was explained in the last section. The polyline will represent the outside of the building area.

Creation Layer for Spaces

If you are using the AIA layer standards set by the Desktop/Drawing Setup, the spaces are created on the A-Area-Spce layer and are colored a brown tone.

Figure 4.8 Spaces toolbar

When you work with space planning, you should switch to the Space layout by picking the Space tab. Your converted polyline will be visible.

To create a space from a polyline, select Spaces/Convert to Spaces from the Concept menu, or select the Convert to Spaces tool from the Spaces toolbar. You'll next be asked to select the polyline to convert. You can then erase the polyline layout or keep it. You'll be presented with the Space Properties dialog box. Under the General tab, you should enter a unique name to describe the space. If you pick the Dimensions tab, you can adjust the space as shown in Figure 4.9.

Remember that spaces are three-dimensional, so you must concern yourself with heights as well as lengths and widths. Refer to the image in the lower left of the dialog box. It helps you relate to the vertical distances. If the vertical dimensions are what you desire, pick OK to create the space. Figure 4.10 shows the newly created space. The plan view shows a cross-hatched area that represents the space. The isometric view shows the floor and ceiling volumes.

TIP: Irregular Spaces

To create an irregular space, you can use any closed polyline. All you need to do is create a closed polyline shape and then turn it into a space.

Figure 4.9 Space Properties dialog box

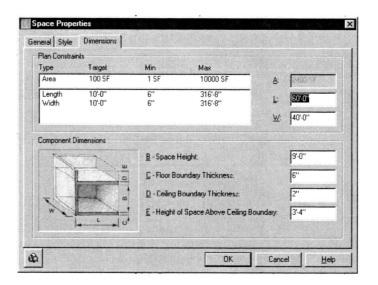

Figure 4.10 Newly created space

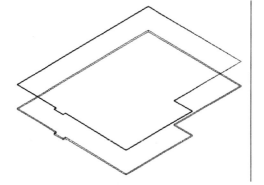

Dividing and Joining Spaces

To create more spaces inside the overall space, you simply divide it up by using either the Divide Spaces tool or by selecting Divide Spaces from the Concept/Spaces pull-down menu. You will be asked to select the space to divide and then to draw a dividing line. This line is used to divide the single space into two spaces. Figure 4.11 shows the space from Figure 4.10 divided into individual spaces. Some of the spaces were joined to create irregular shapes.

You can continue to divide spaces until you have the layout you desire. Later you can convert the spaces into boundaries that are used to represent walls. Figure 4.12 shows the boundaries converted from the spaces. This procedure is explained in the last section of this chapter.

To join spaces together, use the Join Spaces tool. Simply select each space and they'll be joined to create one larger space. Using this method, you can create any shape.

TIP: Dividing Spaces

As a beginner, you will find it useful to divide the spaces where you want a wall to occur. When the boundary (wall) is created, it can use the dividing line between adjoining spaces as the centerline of the wall.

Figure 4.11
Divided spaces

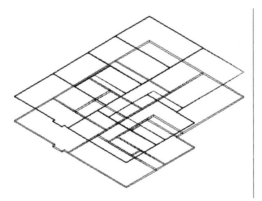
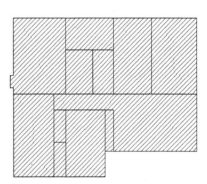

Figure 4.12
Boundaries from spaces

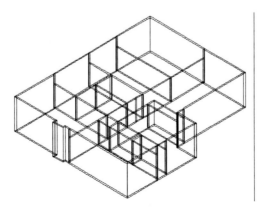
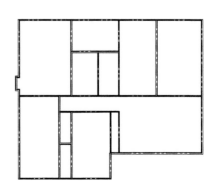

Creating Spaces: Inside-Out

Another approach to space planning is the inside-out method: you create a series of spaces that represent different room areas inside the building; you arrange them in the manner that suits your design; from this arrangement, you create the outside boundaries.

As mentioned before, a space is an object with three dimensions: width, depth, and height. It also can include a representation of the floor boundary and the ceiling boundary, as well as the space above the ceiling boundary. You can create spaces as you go, adjusting the space properties, or you can use customized spaces that have previously been created to suit specific conditions.

To create a simple space, use the Add Spaces tool or select Spaces/Add Space from the Concept pull-down menu. The Add Space dialog box appears as shown in Figure 4.13.

The first setting to notice is the Style drop-down list. By default, it's set to Standard. This is the basic space. You can also make use of specialized styles, but these are not available until you load them. (This procedure will be explained in the next section.)

Referring to Figure 4.13, you can see that you enter the length and width. You can also enter the space height, which can be thought of as the wall height inside the room. There are also two check boxes for the floor boundary and the ceiling boundary. The thickness used for the floor and ceiling boundaries is governed by the space style chosen.

Just as with mass elements, you can place the space and adjust its rotation while the Add Space dialog box is still visible. You can then continue to add spaces until you close the dialog box.

Note that area is also a variable. It is normally locked, but if you have a specific area with which you want to work, you can unlock it. Either the length or the width is then locked. You can then alter the unlocked values, and the locked value is calculated.

The Drag Point button is used to adjust the initial location of the placed space.

A space is an object with three dimensions: width, depth, and height. It also can include a representation of the floor boundary and the ceiling boundary, as well as the space above the ceiling boundary.

Modifying Spaces

You can modify spaces at any time, adjusting their size, shape, or location. You can either pick the Modify Spaces tool, or right-click on the space and choose Space Properties from the context menu.

Space Styles

As mentioned earlier, you can customize space styles to use in different applications. The concept is that you may have preset values for certain spaces and want to apply those preset

Figure 4.13   Add
Space dialog box

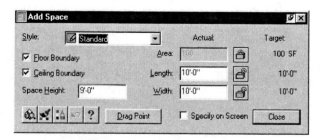

values. As an example, you may want to use several closet spaces with the same size parameters. You can then choose the preset style for closets and place them in the desired locations.

To create, edit, or import/export space styles, pick the Space Styles tool or select Space Styles from the Concept/Spaces pull-down menu. A dialog box similar to Figure 4.14 appears. In a new drawing, a number of space styles are available.

To import styles all you need to do is use the Style Manager's File/Open pull-down menu item. Pick the drawing to open in the Style Manager. All the styles located in the opened drawing will be displayed. Figure 4.14 shows an open Drawing3 that has the typical startup styles and open drawing Spaces - Educational (Imperial). The Spaces - Educational drawing file contains more space styles. To use one of the styles, simply pick from one list and drag to the other. Note the path of the Spaces - Educational styles. By pausing your cursor over an open drawing, the name of the path is displayed. Figure 4.15 shows the folder containing various style drawings.

Figure 4.14 Style Manager dialog box

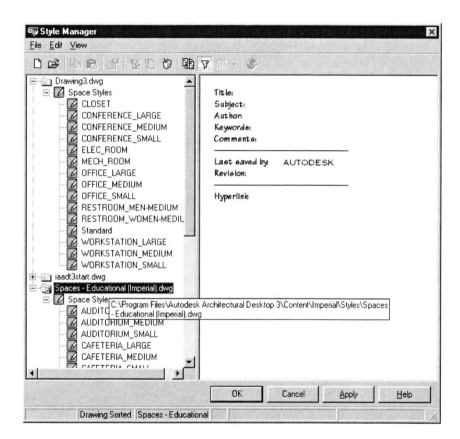

Figure 4.15 Folder containing various style drawings

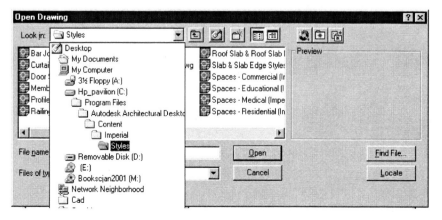

TIP: Creating Your Own Space Styles

Space styles have numerous settings that are operating in the background. One of these is the display system that controls the display of objects that compose a space style. It is usually easier to import an existing space style, modify it for your application, and save it as a new style than it is to create a completely new style.

Once you have imported the various space styles, you can use the Add Space tool to select and place them.

Hands-On: Creating Spaces

In this exercise you'll create a space from a mass model using a polyline and divide the large space into smaller spaces.

1.   Open file ADTEX4B, which contains the office complex from Exercise 4A with a polyline profile created from a floorplate. If you want, you can use your version of the exercise that you saved earlier.

2.   Switch to the Space layout as shown in Figure 4.16. Open the Spaces toolbar.

Converting a Polyline to a Space

3.   Select the Convert to Spaces tool and select the closed polyline. You'll be asked if you want to erase the layout geometry. Reply with a Yes. This will erase the polyline. The Space Properties dialog box appears. Switch to the General tab and enter the name of the space in the description box. In this case, enter Overall. Pick the OK button to create the space using the standard style. Your screen should look like Figure 4.17.

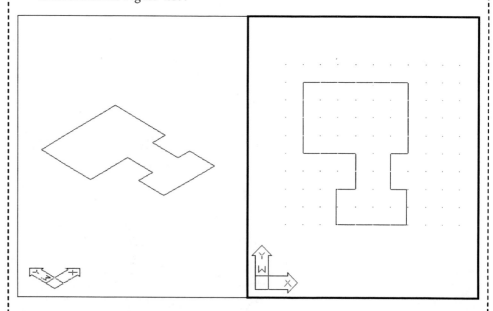

Figure 4.16   Space layout showing polyline

Figure 4.17 Space created from closed polyline

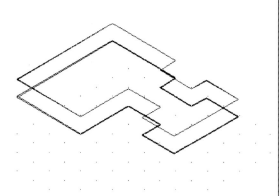
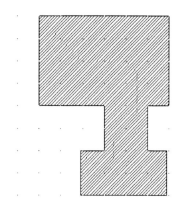

Dividing and Joining Spaces

4. You're going to divide the one large space into three separate spaces. You will do this in two steps.

Pick the Divide Spaces tool and select the large hatched space. You are then asked to identify the divide line start and end points. Refer to Figure 4.18(a) for the location of the points, and use Endpoint object snap to locate the line.

Repeat the procedure to create the new division, as shown in Figure 4.18(b).

5. Create the divisions as shown in Figure 4.19(a), and use the Join Spaces tool to create the space layout shown in Figure 4.19(b).

Figure 4.18
Dividing the one large space into three spaces

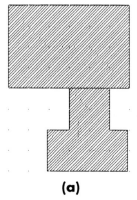
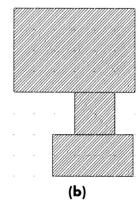

(a)   **(b)**

Figure 4.19 Further divisions and the use of the Join Spaces tool

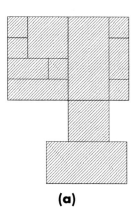
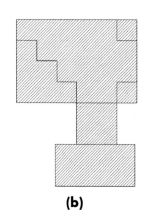

(a)   **(b)**

Adding a Space

Since the space planning is now separated from the mass model, you can add spaces even on the exterior to create a new exterior profile. In this step, you're going to add a preset space style to add a space.

6. Pick the Space Styles tool and pick Open from the File pull-down menu.
    Use Lookin: to open the Styles folder. Refer to Figure 4.20 to make sure you're in the right folder. Highlight the Spaces - Commercial (Imperial).dwg file and open it. This contains the preset styles for a commercial application.
    Open the Space Styles tree under the Spaces - Commercial heading. Highlight CONFERENCE_LARGE and drag it into the Space Styles heading on your current drawing. Once it has been imported, pick the OK buttons until all the dialog boxes are closed.

7. Pick the Add Spaces tool and open the Style drop-down list. The style CONFERENCE_LARGE should be listed. Pick it to make it current. The dialog box settings should have changed to match the current style (see Figure 4.21). Your settings should be similar.
    Place the new space as shown in Figure 4.22 and close the dialog box.

8. Save your drawing file as EX4B.

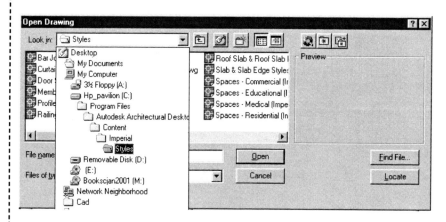

Figure 4.20   Folder containing space styles

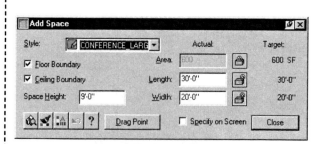

Figure 4.21   Add Space dialog box showing CONFERENCE_LARGE style

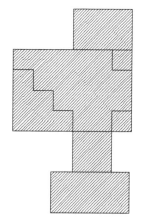

Figure 4.22   New space placed on the exterior of building

Space Boundaries

A space boundary is a division between spaces that may exist as a solid-form boundary or as an area-separation boundary. Solid boundaries can be thought of as walls with a specified thickness. They have all the characteristics of a wall such as justification, base height, and thickness and can eventually be turned into actual walls in your model. Area-separation boundaries have no thickness and are used as symbolic dividers between spaces where no actual wall would exist. For example, in an open office complex, different departments may be allocated various spaces, even though no actual walls exist between the areas. To keep these areas separate, an area-separation boundary is used.

Space boundaries appear as cyan-colored (light blue) lines. If they're solid-form boundaries, they're displayed as two lines separated by a thickness with a centerline running between. If a boundary is an area separation, the cyan-colored line overlaps the brown line of the space perimeter. In the AIA layer naming system, the space boundaries are created on the A-Area-Bdry layer. Figure 4.23(a) shows a close-up view of the solid-form space boundary. Figure 4.23(b) shows the Space Boundaries toolbar.

Creation of Space Boundaries

To create an individual space boundary, use the Add Boundary tool, or select Space Boundaries/Add Boundary from the Concepts pull-down menu. A dialog box similar to Figure 4.24 appears.

The Segment Type controls whether the boundary is a solid form or an area separation.

The Manage Contained Spaces box creates a space associated with the boundary. If a boundary is created with spaces, and the spaces were to be erased, the boundaries would be erased as well.

You can specify the height, width, justification, and offset. Justification is used to specify whether the wall runs along the left, right, or center of the picked points. Offset is

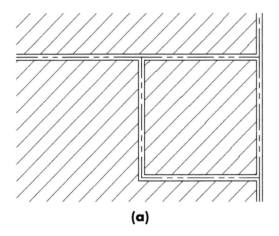

(a)

(b)

Figure 4.23   (a) Solid-form space boundary; (b) Space Boundaries toolbar

Figure 4.24   Add Space Boundary dialog box

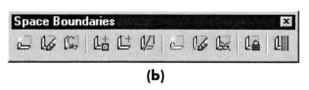

TIP: Creation Layer for Boundary Spaces

If you are using the AIA layer standards set by the Desktop/Drawing Setup, the boundary spaces are created on the A-Area-Bdry layer and are colored cyan (light blue).

used to draw the wall a specified distance away from the points you pick. Boundaries can be created as straight lines or arcs.

Solid boundaries can be thought of as walls with a specified thickness; separation boundaries have no thickness and are used as symbolic dividers between spaces.

After you've picked at least three points, the Ortho Close and Polyline Close buttons become accessible. Ortho closes the space by drawing two walls or space boundaries based on the direction you specify. Polyline closes the wall by creating a wall segment from the last point specified to the first point specified for the group of walls.

You can modify space boundary properties after they've been created. This procedure is explained in a later section of this chapter.

Adding Boundary Edges

You can add new boundary edges to existing boundaries. The additional boundary edge becomes integrated into the existing boundary.

To add a new boundary, use the Add Boundary Edges tool, or select Space Boundaries/Add Boundary Edges from the Concept pull-down menu. First, specify the existing boundary and then draw the new boundary edges.

Remember that the start and the end points for the boundary edge must touch the spaces inside the existing boundaries in order to form a new space within the added edges. Figure 4.25 shows the addition of a boundary edge.

Merging Boundaries

You can merge two or more boundaries to make one space. Select the Merge Boundaries tool, or select Space Boundaries/Merge Boundaries from the Concept pull-down menu.

Figure 4.25   Adding a boundary edge

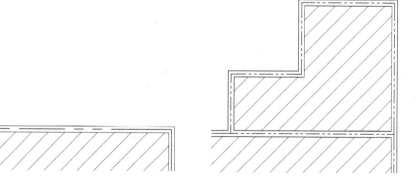

You will first be asked to identify the boundary of the space to be enlarged and then the second boundary to merge with the first. The two boundaries will then become one larger boundary.

Removing Boundary Edges

You can remove a boundary edge from an existing space boundary. Select the Remove Boundary Edges tool, or select Space Boundaries/Remove Boundary Edges from the Concept pull-down menu.

If the space boundary also contained a space, the space is erased because the space boundary is now open where the boundary edge was removed.

Converting Objects to Boundaries

You can create space boundaries by converting spaces, slices, polylines, arcs, and lines. Select the Concept/Space Boundaries/Convert to Boundaries pull-down menu. There are three choices: edge, space, and slice.

You can convert two or more nonoverlapping spaces to create one space boundary that surrounds each space object. Even if the boundaries are not connected, they're still considered the same space boundary.

If you want to convert a slice to a space boundary, it must have objects attached to it.

When you convert edge objects such as polylines, arcs, and lines to boundaries, you have the option of erasing the original sketching objects when the boundaries are created.

Modifying Space Boundaries

You can modify the entire space boundary or individual boundary edges. To modify the entire space boundary, select the Modify Boundary tool, or select Space Boundaries/ Modify Boundary from the Concept pull-down menu. Pick the space boundary you wish to modify. A dialog box similar to Figure 4.26 appears. If you want to change more detailed properties of the boundary, pick the Properties tool located in the lower left of

TIP: Space Boundary Properties
of Converted Objects

When you convert an object such as a space, slice, or polyline into a space boundary, it takes on the default space boundary properties such as height, width (wall thickness), ceiling, and floor space. You should use the Modify Boundary tool to check the properties of the newly created boundary to see if the settings match what you want.

Figure 4.26 Modify Space Boundary dialog box

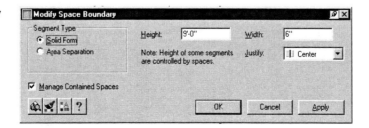

Figure 4.27 Space
Boundary Properties
dialog box showing
Design Rules tab active

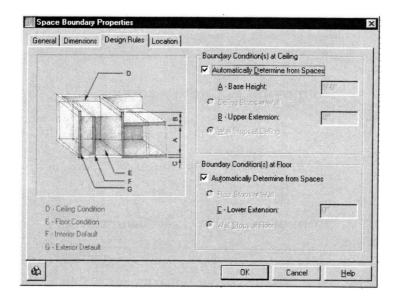

the dialog box. The Space Boundary Properties dialog box appears, similar to Figure 4.27. Using this dialog box, you can modify the design rules as shown in Figure 4.27. This is useful when you want to add ceiling and floor spaces.

To modify an individual existing boundary edge, select the Edit Boundary Edges tool, or select Space Boundaries/Edit Boundary Edges from the Concept pull-down menu. You'll be asked to identify the boundary edge to modify. A dialog box similar to Figure 4.28 appears.

You can create space boundaries by converting spaces, slices, polylines, arcs, and lines.

Figure 4.28
Boundary Edge
Properties dialog box

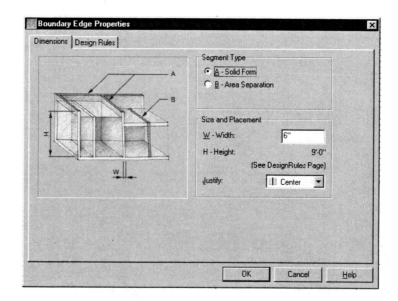

Hands-On: Creating Space Boundaries

In this exercise you'll create space boundaries by several methods, including converting, adding, and removing.

1.   Open file ADTEX4C, which contains the spaces you created in ADTEX4B. If you want, you can use your version of the exercise that you saved earlier. Make sure that the Space tab is active, and display the Space Boundaries toolbar.

Converting Spaces to Space Boundaries

2.   Open the Concept pull-down menu and select Space Boundaries/Convert to Boundaries and enter SP to select spaces. When asked to select spaces, window around all the spaces. A single space boundary is created. The boundary edges are hard to see because they have been created as area-separation boundaries. You may be able to notice the cyan-colored lines overlapping the space perimeters.

Modifying the Space Boundary

3.   You're going to modify the properties of the space boundary to turn the edges into solid forms that resemble walls. Select the Modify Boundary tool, pick one of the boundary edges, and press Enter to continue. A Modify Space Boundary dialog box similar to Figure 4.29 appears. Change the Segment Type to Solid Form, and make sure the width is set to 6″ and the justification to Center. Pick the Apply button and observe the results. The area-separation boundaries changed to 6″-wide solid-form boundaries. Pick the OK button to complete the command. Figure 4.30 shows the results of the modification. Note how the isometric view now shows the solid-form walls.

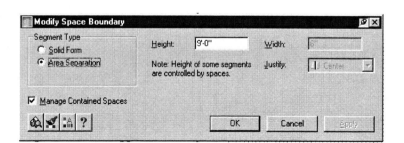

Figure 4.29   Modify Space Boundary dialog box

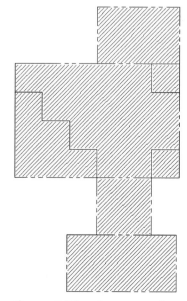

Figure 4.30   Area-separation boundaries changed to solid-form boundaries

Adding a Boundary Edge

4.   Zoom in on the plan as shown in Figure 4.31(a). Select the Add Boundary Edges tool. You'll be asked to select the space boundary. Refer to Figure 4.31(a) and pick one of the boundary edges to which you'll add the new boundary. Once you've picked the existing space boundary, the Add Space Boundary dialog box appears. Its settings will match those of the existing boundary that you picked. Draw the solid-form boundary as shown in Figure 4.31(b). The key to adding edges is to make sure that their start and end points overlap the existing boundary. Once you've picked the start and end points, press Enter to add the edge. The results should look like Figure 4.31(b). If you picked the correct points, the boundary joints should clean up automatically.

Removing a Boundary Edge

5.   While still zoomed in, highlight each of the visible spaces by picking them one at a time. Note that each space inside a space boundary is a separate space. Press the Esc key several times until no spaces are highlighted.

6.   Use the Remove Boundary Edge tool to erase the boundary edge shown in Figure 4.32. When you open a boundary, the joining spaces become one. Pick

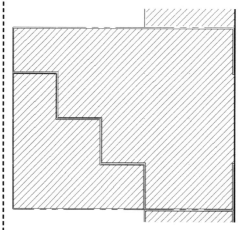
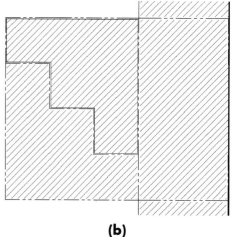

(a)   (b)

Figure 4.31   New space boundary

Figure 4.32
Removing a boundary
edge

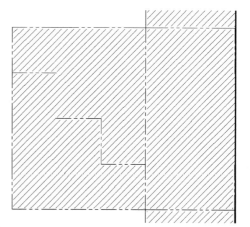

one of the spaces that was separated by the edge you removed. Note that the two spaces are now one.

7.   Use the Add Boundary Edge tool to add the edge back in.

8.   Save your file as EX4C.

In a Nutshell

You should now have an understanding of the different methods of creating the interior conceptual design, using floorplates, space planning, and space boundaries.

You can initially base the interior conceptual design on the exterior conceptual design through the mass model, but once you start creating spaces and boundaries, the link disappears. If you want, you can jump right to space planning and boundary creation and skip the exterior mass model altogether. It's up to you how creative you want to be with your design.

The next stage is design development, which is the refinement of the design with the generation of walls, columns, and roofs. This topic is covered in the next chapter.

 # Testing... testing... 1, 2, 3

Short Answer

1. What are the two ways to create a slice marker?

a._____

b._____

2. a. Solid boundaries are displayed as_____

_____

b. Area separations are displayed as_____

_____

3. To merge two or more boundaries to make one space:

a._____

b._____

4. Once you have created the mass model, you can slice the model horizontally to create _____ profiles. These profiles are referred to as _____.

5. The final link between the mass model and space planning is _____

_____

Multiple Choice

6. To access most of the spacing planning commands, you use the

a. Spaces toolbar.

b. PLAN command.

c. SPACES command.

d. Mass Element toolbar.

e. a and c

7. To create more spaces inside the overall space, you simply divide it up by
    a. typing Divide Spaces on the command line.
    b. using the Divide Spaces tool.
    c. selecting Divide Spaces from the Concepts/Spaces pull-down menu.
    d. all the above
    e. b and c
8. You can modify spaces at any time, adjusting their
    a. shape, frequency, or density.
    b. size, shape, or location.
    c. angle, constancy, adaptability.
    d. all the above
    e. a and b

True or False

9. Area-separation boundaries have all the characteristics of a wall such as justification, base height, and thickness and can eventually be turned into actual walls in your model.   T or F
10. If you want to convert a slice to a space boundary, it must have objects attached to it. T or F

What?

1. What is the purpose of having access to various space styles?
2. Identify and explain the differences between the two types of space boundaries.
3. How can you change the elevation of a slice?
4. Explain the procedure for making a polyline reflect a change in the floorplate.
5. What is the procedure used to divide a space into two spaces?

Let's Get Busy!

1. Using Assignment 2 of Chapter 3, Let's Get Busy, create a single floorplate to show the exterior of the building. Convert the floorplate to a polyline, and convert the polyline into a single space. Using Spaces and space boundaries, create the layout shown in Figure 4.33. The actual sizes of the rooms are not important, only that they be proportional to the layout. Use a wall width/thickness of 6 inches.

2. Using Assignment 3 of Chapter 3, Let's Get Busy, create two floorplates to show the exterior of the building. Place the floorplate at 11 feet above the ground level. Convert the floorplate to a polyline. Use the polyline as the exterior shell. Offset the exterior polyline 3 feet, to create an interior polyline as shown in Figure 4.34. Convert the interior polyline to a space object using Spaces and space boundaries to create an original layout. You may want to import space styles to generate the room. Use an interior wall width/thickness of 6 inches.

Figure 4.33 Interior space planning of bungalow

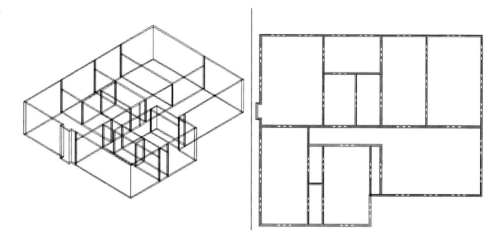

Figure 4.34 Addition of interior polyline used to create space object

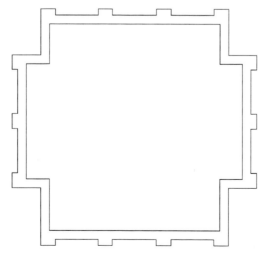

Chapter 5
Design Development

Yesterday and Today

The house at the top was built in the 1600s, the one below it in 1996. They are next to each other on the same block. Like many neighborhoods in many worldwide communities, this development in Inverness, Scotland, wishes to protect the architectural integrity of the nearby area by requiring that the styles of new houses be similar to those of their older neighbors.

Key Concepts

- Walls
- Columns and Grids
- Sloped Roofs

Design Development

In the design development stage you start to add more detail to your design; you take the conceptual and make it more concrete. The first steps in design development are to choose and apply wall styles, to place column grids to identify the building's structural system, and to design a roof. Once these tasks are completed, you can start to add various components such as doors, windows, stairs, and so on.

Once you're comfortable with Architectural Desktop, you'll find yourself jumping back and forth through the design process. Don't feel that the pedagogy of this book has to limit your creative intuition. Your approach may be to design the roof before you have walls to support it. The great thing about Architectural Desktop is that you can most certainly do this, if that's what you desire.

Walls

Although walls are among the most complex objects created in Architectural Desktop, because they contain all the geometry necessary to represent a wall in 2D and 3D views, including edges and surfaces, you may find them the easiest to manipulate because of their built-in intelligence.

There are two types of walls—wall objects and curtain wall objects.

A curtain wall object is similar to a wall object in its placement and modification. The difference is that it's composed of a grid that contains various types of panels. This is explained in more detail in Appendix B. This chapter deals with the application of wall objects.

A wall also may be composed of a variety of materials, adding to its complexity. Thankfully, there are precreated wall styles from which to choose. These can be used as a starting point from which to create other styles, which greatly reduces the complexity of the task and the time it takes to create them from scratch.

Additionally there is automatic cleanup between intersecting walls. You're able to control many of the cleanup characteristics, from the proximity of the walls to the cleanup of only similarly composed walls.

Once you're comfortable with Architectural Desktop, you'll find yourself jumping back and forth through the design process.

Figure 5.1 Walls toolbar

TIP: Creation Layer for Walls

If you're using the AIA layer standards set by the Desktop/Drawing setup, the walls are created on the A-Wall layer and are yellow.

As you'll find out later, behaviors of other objects are controlled by the placement of walls. For instance, doors and windows are controlled by the wall on which they are placed. They can move along the wall but cannot move outside the structure of the wall. This is certainly sensible behavior for doors and windows.

The Walls toolbar contains most of the wall commands (see Figure 5.1). There is also a Wall Tools toolbar that contains more advanced commands to modify a wall object. This is explained further in this chapter.

There are three methods for creating walls. The first method is to add walls directly to represent the building layout. The second method is to convert the standard drawing objects—lines, arcs, circles, or polylines—to walls. The third method is to convert space boundaries to walls. We'll begin by discussing the direct method of adding walls.

Adding Walls

To create a wall, select the Add Wall tool, or select Walls/Add Wall from the Design pull-down menu. You'll be presented with an Add Walls dialog box similar to Figure 5.2(a). The first important item in the dialog box is the Style drop-down list. Picking it presents you with a list of wall styles loaded into the drawing (see Figure 5.2(b)). If you use the start-up drawing for this text or the template file for Architectural Desktop, you'll find that a series of precreated wall styles have already been loaded.

A wall style is composed of a series of components that represent the construction of the wall. They can be as simple as two lines that represent the Standard style or more complex, such as the Stud-4 Rigid-1.5 Air-1 Brick-4 wall style that is composed of 4" brick, 1" air space, $1\frac{1}{2}$" rigid insulation, 4" stud, and $\frac{5}{8}$" wallboard. Figure 5.3 shows partial walls in the plan view of the Standard and Stud-4 Rigid-1.5 Air-1 Brick-4 wall styles. You can create your own wall styles, but for now we'll use the ones already made for us.

The next item to notice in the Add Walls dialog box is the Group drop-down list. This setting is used to apply automatic cleanup of intersecting walls. Basically, a cleanup group controls the behavior of two intersecting walls, such as which components take precedence over other components (which objects will be trimmed, which will remain).

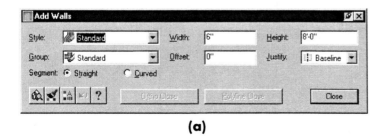

(a)

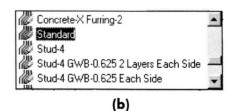

(b)

Figure 5.2   Add Walls dialog box and a partial list of wall styles

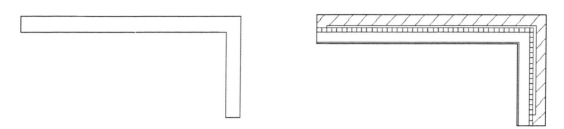

Figure 5.3   Partial walls using the Standard and the Stud-4 Rigid-1.5 Air-1 Brick-4 wall styles

Initially there is only the Standard cleanup group. You can create very sophisticated cleanup groups for complex walls. For now, we'll stick with the Standard cleanup group.

If you select the Standard wall style, you can enter any wall thickness you want. If you select one of the other wall styles, the wall thickness will have been preset. Some wall styles have an X in their name, such as Stud-X. This means that you can adjust the thickness of the stud.

You can adjust the wall height for any wall type, and once the wall is created, you'll be able to modify its height to accommodate sloped ceilings or floors.

The Offset value is used to draw the wall a specified distance from the points picked for the start and end of the wall.

The Justify drop-down list gives you four choices: Left, Right, Center, and Baseline. This setting can be important depending on whether the wall is interior or exterior and how many components it comprises.

The Segment area controls whether the section of wall is straight or curved.

Drawing the Wall

When you activate the Add Walls dialog box, a wall segment appears on your drawing at 0,0. This indicates the start point of the line. When you pick the actual location of the line, the segment moves to the new location. As you drag the cursor the length of the wall forms. You'll notice a right-triangle icon appear as you draw. This is used to indicate the direction in which you're drawing. The triangle points toward the end of the wall. This feature can be important with complex walls composed of several materials. It controls how the components in the wall are assembled. If after you have drawn the wall the material is on the wrong side, you can reverse the drawing direction of the wall, thereby reversing the sides on which the materials are situated. Figure 5.4 shows the creation of a wall segment. Note that Polar snap was turned on so that the length of the wall segment was displayed during creation.

You can undo the creation points of a wall as you draw it, but you cannot undo the starting point. Press the Esc key to abort the command and start over.

When drawing curved walls, you specify the start point, the midpoint of the curve, and the endpoint. You can switch back and forth between straight and curved walls as you're placing location points.

Use the Match Properties tool in the Add Walls dialog box to match the properties of the new wall you're creating with those of an existing wall in your drawing.

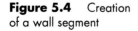

Figure 5.4   Creation of a wall segment

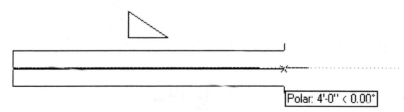

Polar: 4'-0" < 0.00°

TIP: Reversing the Wall Material Construction

If you draw a wall, and the materials composing a wall are on the wrong side, you can remedy this situation by reversing the direction of the wall. To change the direction of an existing wall, right-click on the wall, and select Plan Tools/Reverse from the context menu. The materials then switch to the opposite side of the wall.

Modifying Walls

You can change any characteristic of a wall using the Modify Wall tool. Select the tool and pick a single wall segment to modify, or pick several to change at once. The Modify Walls dialog box appears as shown in Figure 5.5. You can easily change any of the standard size values or the wall style itself.

To alter the shape of the wall, pick the Properties tool in the Modify Walls dialog box. You'll be presented with a dialog box similar to Figure 5.6. This allows you to modify any property of a selected wall. To change the shape of the wall, pick the Roof/Floor Line tab, and the dialog box changes to look like Figure 5.7.

Refer to the Vertex Editing window located in the Roof/Wall Line dialog box shown in Figure 5.7. The box shapes at the corners are vertices used to define the shape of the wall. There are vertices for the roof and vertices for the floor. To access either the roof or floor vertices, pick either the Edit Roof Line or the Edit Floor Line box. To alter the vertex location, pick it to highlight it, and then use the Edit Vertex button.

Figure 5.5 Modify Walls dialog box

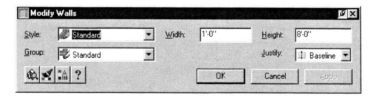

Figure 5.6 Wall Properties dialog box

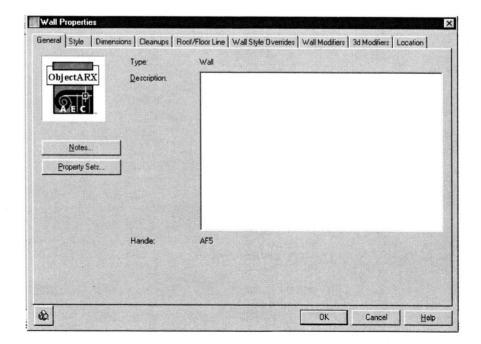

Figure 5.7 Wall Properties dialog box with the Roof/Floor Line tab active

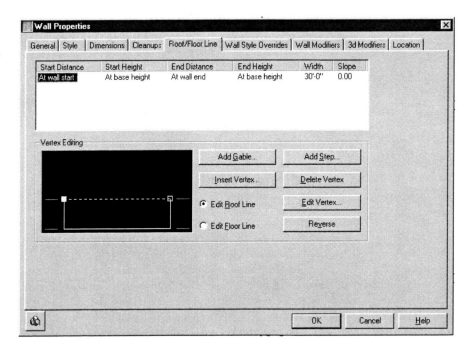

TIP: Modifying Wall Thickness

You can modify most of a wall's properties. However, if you use a wall style other than Standard or a name containing an "X," you cannot change the wall thickness. This thickness is set when the wall style is created. You have to change the wall style in order to change the wall's thickness.

You can change any characteristic of a wall using the Modify Wall tool.

To add a gable, pick the Add Gable button, and a third vertex is added to the roof line set halfway between the two ends of the roof line and 8 feet up from the roof line (see Figure 5.8). You can adjust the location of the gable vertex using the Edit Vertex button.

To add a step in the roof or the floor, pick the Add Step button.

Converting Objects to Walls

You can convert lines, arcs, circles, or polylines to walls by using the Convert to Walls tool. The walls take on the Standard wall style, and you can modify them when the Wall Properties dialog box appears.

You can also convert Space Boundaries to walls by selecting Generate Walls from the Concept/Space Boundaries pull-down menu.

Wall Styles

If you select the Wall Styles tool or the Design/Walls/Wall Styles pull-down menu, you'll be presented with a dialog box similar to Figure 5.9.

Figure 5.8 Adding a gable

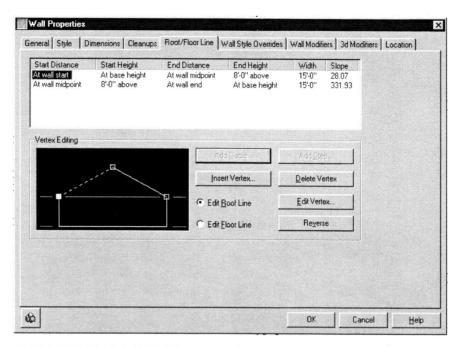

Figure 5.9 Style Manager dialog box

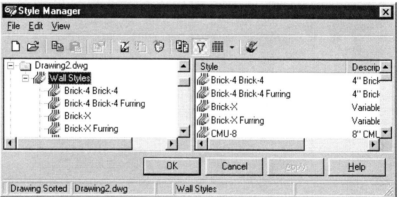

If you use the startup file from this text or the Architectural Desktop template file, you'll have access to all the precreated wall styles. It is much easier for a beginner to make use of the previously created ones.

To import styles, all you need to do is use the Style Manager's File/Open pull-down menu item. You then can pick the drawing to open in the Style Manager. All the styles located in the opened drawing are displayed. Figure 5.9 shows an open Drawing1 that has the typical startup wall styles and open drawing Wall Styles - Casework (Imperial). The Wall Styles - Casework drawing file contains more wall styles. To use one of the styles, simply pick from one list and drag to the other. Figure 5.10 shows the path to the folder containing various styles drawings.

Figure 5.10 Path to locating the wall styles

Hands-On: Creating Walls

In this exercise you'll practice creating walls and modifying wall segments to change their shapes.

1.   Open start-up file iaad3start and immediately save it as EX5A.

2.   Display the Walls toolbar and pick the Work-3D layout tab. Turn Snap and Ortho on.

Creating Walls

3.   Select the Add Wall tool, and the dialog box should appear. Set the width of the wall to 12″ so that you can see it more easily as you create it. Your dialog box should look similar to Figure 5.11. Start the wall at 0,0 and draw it 30′ long along the positive X axis. Continue to draw it upward 20′ along the Y axis. Now, draw it 30′ back along the negative X axis, and pick the Polyline Close button. You should have a rectangle of walls that looks similar to Figure 5.12.

Modifying Walls

4.   You're going to change the shape of the 20-foot walls. Select the Modify Wall tool and select one of the 20-foot walls in the plan view and press Enter to display the Wall Modify dialog box.

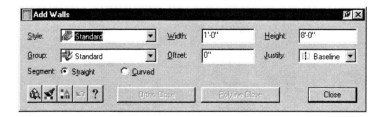

Figure 5.11   Add Walls dialog

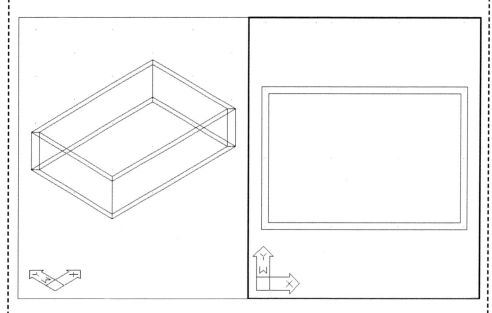

Figure 5.12   Thirty- and 20-foot-long walls

Pick the Properties tool to display the Wall Properties dialog box. Pick the Roof/Floor Line tab. Pick the Add Gable button. Your dialog box should look similar to Figure 5.13. Pick the box that represents the vertex of the gable and then pick the Edit Vertex button. Change Distance to 5′ and pick OK. The dialog box should now look like Figure 5.14. Pick OK to exit the dialog box. Repeat for the other 20-foot wall. Refer to a 3D view of the walls. Note the addition of the gables as shown in Figure 5.15.

5. Save your file as EX5A.

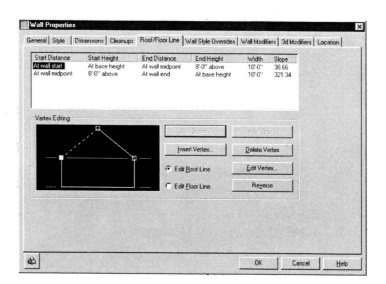

Figure 5.13   Adding a gable to the wall

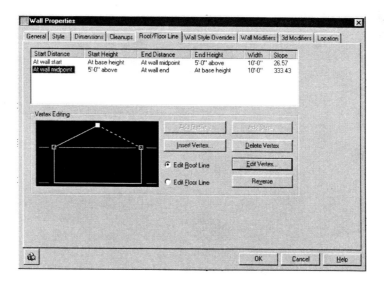

Figure 5.14   Changing the gable distance to 5 feet

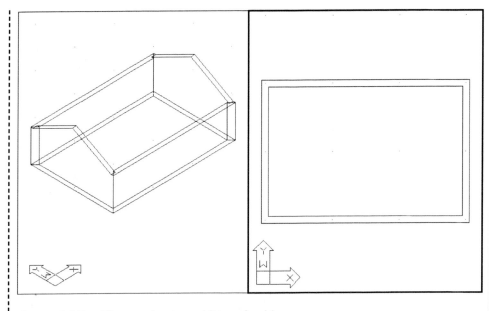

Figure 5.15   3D view showing addition of gables

Wall Cleanup Groups

Whenever two walls intersect each other, a wall cleanup group is applied. The purpose of the cleanup group is to control how the wall components are trimmed or extended automatically. Walls that intersect with the same cleanup group are trimmed or extended; walls that intersect with different cleanup groups won't affect each other.

By default, walls are created using the Standard cleanup group. This setting has the effect of cleaning up all walls with other walls. You can create your own cleanup group, thereby controlling how walls clean up with each other. When you create or modify walls, you can use different cleanup group names to control the cleanup.

 Before you can apply a cleanup group to a wall you must create it first. This is done using the Style Manager dialog box. If you pick the Cleanup Group Definitions tool or select Walls/Wall Cleanup Group Definitions from the Design pull-down menu, you'll be presented with the Style Manager dialog box. If you right-click on the Cleanup Group Definitions heading under your current drawing, a context menu will appear. Pick New from this menu and a new style is created. If you right-click on the new style name and pick Edit from the context menu you can alter the properties of the new style.

Once you have a new cleanup group, you can apply it to a wall; this is done by modifying the properties of the wall. Figure 5.16(a) shows two sets of intersecting walls. The first set has the same wall cleanup group name. The second set has two different wall cleanup group names. Note the difference in the intersections.

Figure 5.16(b) shows the Cleanup Settings for a selected wall. You can set the cleanup radius, set which cleanup group to use, or pick to which end of the wall you want to apply a

TIP: Organizing Wall Cleanup Groups

You may want to create a series of standards for wall cleanup groups. You can store them in a single drawing and import them into a current drawing whenever necessary.

Figure 5.16 (a) Matching and different wall cleanup groups and (b) Cleanup Settings

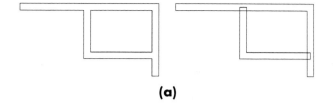

(a)

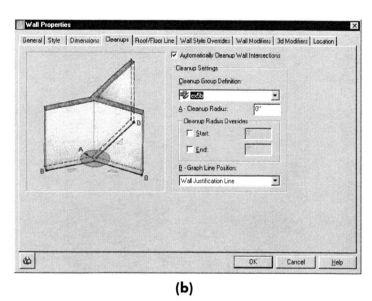

(b)

cleanup radius. The cleanup radius determines how close a wall has to be to another wall before it is cleaned up. You can adjust this size up and down until you get the desired effect on two intersecting walls.

Wall Tools

Once you have drawn a wall, you can use a variety of advanced commands to alter the appearance of the wall. These tools have been assembled into one toolbar called Wall Tools (see Figure 5.17).

Wall Endcaps

Wall endcaps control the appearance of termination points on walls. An endcap is a polyline shape that is placed on either end of a wall segment. By default, the BYSTYLE wall endcap is applied to all walls. To override an endcap, select the wall, right-click, and pick Wall Properties from the context menu. Open the Wall Style Overrides tab, and pick either Start Endcap or End Endcap. A dialog box similar to Figure 5.18 appears. You can then pick the style from the list.

To create an endcap style, pick the Endcap Styles tool and the Style Manager dialog box. The procedure to create an endcap style name is the same as explained earlier in the creation of a cleanup group.

Figure 5.17   Wall Tools toolbar

Figure 5.18 Select an Endcap Style dialog box

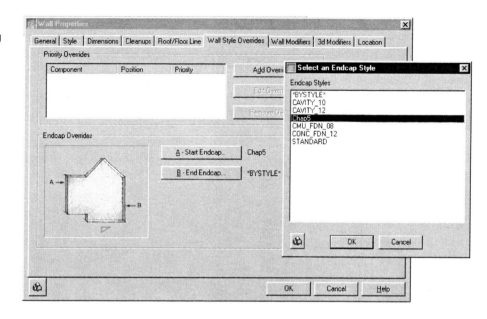

To apply a polyline shape to an endcap style, highlight the new style name and select Edit/Set From from the pull-down menu as shown in Figure 5.19. You'll be asked to select a polyline. Once you pick it, you'll be asked for a component index number to assign to that segment. Enter 1 for a simple standard wall. Complex walls can be composed of several components, such as brick, air space, and so on. Each one of these components is assigned a component index number. The purpose is so that each endcap polyline segment can be assigned a component index matching the wall component. Figure 5.20 shows the polyline and the effect on the ends of a wall.

Figure 5.19 Applying a polyline to an endcap style

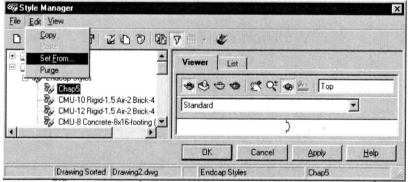

Figure 5.20 Polyline used as an endcap

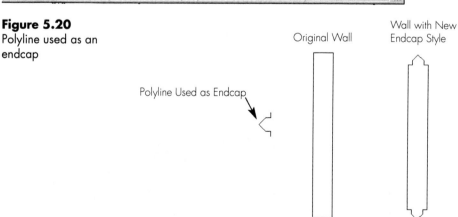

Wall Modifier Styles

A wall modifier style adds components to a wall to further define its features. You do this by drawing a polyline to represent the feature and then creating a new wall modifier style that uses the polyline.

The procedure to create a wall modifier is the same as the endcap style. Create a new style name and then set/apply a polyline to the name. Figure 5.21(a) shows the polyline and its effect on the ends of a wall.

To add a wall modifier to a wall segment, select the wall, right-click, and pick Wall Properties from the context menu. Open the Wall Modifiers tab and pick the Add button. Then pick the style from the list. Adjust the parameters as shown in Figure 5.21(b).

You can also use the Add Wall Modifier tool to add a wall modifier. The procedure is the same as using the wall properties except it uses a separate dialog box.

3D Modifiers

There are three types of 3D modifiers: wall interference, wall sweep, and wall body. These are used to further modify a wall by using existing objects.

Wall interference allows you to place AEC objects, such as mass elements, in walls to create custom openings.

Wall sweep allows you to define a polyline profile and use that shape as the shape of a wall component. The insertion point of the profile is used as the lower-left corner of the wall component.

Wall body allows you to replace an entire wall or a component in the wall with a mass element or an AEC object with mass.

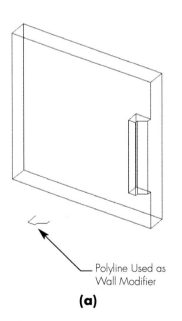

(a)

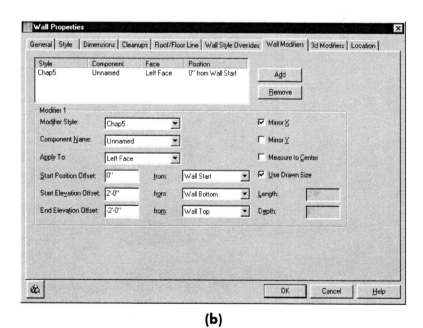

(b)

Figure 5.21   (a) Polyline used as a wall modifier and (b) Wall Modifiers tab

Hands-On: Editing a Wall

In this exercise you'll practice applying wall cleanup groups, wall endcap styles, and wall modifier styles.

1.   Open file adtex5B, which contains walls, and polylines to be used as endcaps and wall modifiers. Save it as EX5B.

2.   Display the Walls toolbar and pick the Work-3D layout tab.

Creating a Wall Cleanup Group

3.   Select Cleanup Group Definitions from the Design/Walls pull-down menu. The Group Cleanup Definitions dialog box appears. Right-click the Cleanup Group Definitions heading in the ex5b drawing and pick New from the context menu. Enter EX5B as the new style name. Highlight the name in the list of style names and right-click. Select Edit from the context menu. Enter Chapter 5 Wall Cleanup Group in the Description box, and pick OK. The dialog box should look like Figure 5.22. Pick OK to exit the dialog box.

4.   Select the Modify Wall tool, select all the interior walls, and press Enter. Change the group to EX5B as shown in Figure 5.23. Pick the Apply button to see the effect, and then pick OK to close the dialog box. Figure 5.24 shows the results. Because the interior walls are now in their own wall cleanup group, they don't cut into the exterior walls.

Creating a Wall Endcap Style

5.   The first step is to create the wall endcap style. Open the Wall Tools toolbar and select the Wall Endcap Styles tool. The Endcap Styles dialog box appears.
Right-click the Endcap Styles heading in the ex5b drawing and pick New from the context menu. Enter EX5B as the new style name. Highlight the name

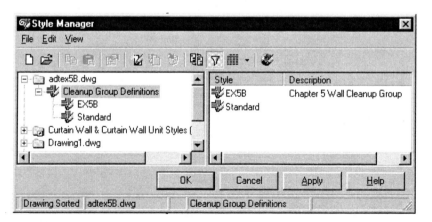

Figure 5.22   Style Manager dialog box showing Cleanup Group Definitions

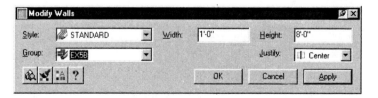

Figure 5.23   Modify Walls dialog box showing the change in the group

Figure 5.24   Results of different wall cleanup groups

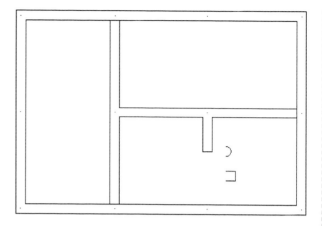

in the list of style names and right-click. Select Edit from the context menu. Enter Chapter 5 Wall Endcap Style in the Description box, and pick OK to exit.

To apply a polyline shape to an endcap style, highlight the EX5B style name and select Edit/Set From from the pull-down menu. You'll be asked to select a polyline. Normally, you would have already drawn the polyline shape you want to use as the endcap. In this exercise, we have drawn one for you. Pick the arc polyline. You are asked to enter a component index for this segment. Enter 1. You will next be asked if you want to add another component. Enter No. Enter a return offset of 0. Figure 5.25 shows the dialog box. Pick OK to exit the dialog box.

Before you continue, we will explain some of the previous settings. A wall can comprise different components. Each component is given an index number. When you select a polyline for an endcap, you're asked the component index number. This controls the component of the wall to which the endcap is applied. A wall endcap with a component index of 1 is added only to a wall component that has the same index.

You can add more than one polyline component to an endcap style and assign different index values to each one.

Applying a Wall Endcap Style

6.   Pick the short protruding wall to highlight it, and right-click to bring up the context menu. Select Wall Properties from the list. When the Wall Properties dialog box appears, select the Wall Style Overrides tab. Pick the B - End Endcap button and select EX5B from the list. Pick the OK button to accept the endcap style. You should now see the word EX5B next to the B - End Endcap

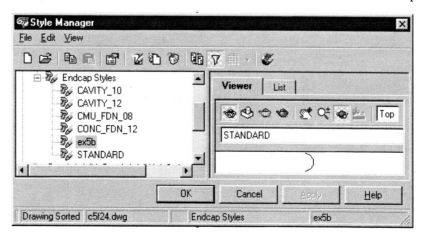

Figure 5.25   Style Manager dialog box showing wall endcap styles

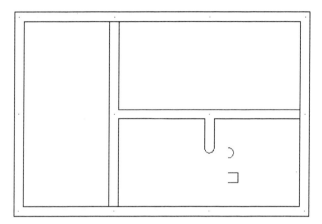

Figure 5.26   Results of new endcap style

button. Pick the OK button to exit the dialog box. The end of the wall should now appear similar to Figure 5.26.

Creating a Wall Modifier Style

7.   The procedure for creating a wall modifier style is practically the same as that for creating a wall endcap style. Select the Wall Modifier Styles tool. The Wall Modifier Styles dialog box appears.

Right-click the Wall Modifier Styles heading in the ex5b drawing and pick New from the context menu. Enter EX5B as the new style name. Highlight the name in the list of style names and right-click. Select Edit from the context menu. Enter Chapter 5 Wall Modifier Style in the Description box, and pick OK to exit.

To apply a polyline shape to a wall modifier style, highlight the EX5B style name and select Edit/Set From from the pull-down menu. You'll be asked to select a polyline. Normally you would have already drawn the polyline shape you want to use as the wall modifier. In this exercise, we have drawn one for you. Pick the open box-shaped polyline. Figure 5.27 shows the dialog box. Pick OK to exit the dialog box.

Applying a Wall Modifier Style

8.   Pick the interior wall (vertical) to highlight it, and right-click to bring up the context menu. Select Wall Properties from the list. When the Wall Properties dialog box appears, select the Wall Modifiers tab. Pick the Add button and select EX5B from the Modifier Style list. All the settings should now have turned from gray to black to allow access.

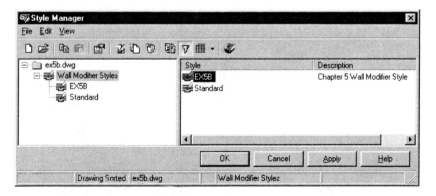

Figure 5.27   Style Manager dialog box showing Wall Modifier Styles

Pick the Floating Viewer button to display a window showing the wall. In the viewer, set the view to SW Isometric (see Figure 5.28). The Floating Viewer shows the effects of the settings before they're applied to the wall. The protrusion on the end of the wall is the EX5B wall modifier.

Refer to the settings and note that the Apply To box is set to Both Faces. Change the setting to Left Face and observe the results in the Floating Viewer.

Now, enter 5′ in the Length box and 1′ in the Depth box. Watch the results in the Floating Viewer as you enter the values.

Enter 2′ in the Start Position Offset box and observe the results. Enter 3′ in the Start Elevation Offset box and observe the results. Return the Start Elevation Offset to 0.

Set the End Elevation Offset box to 5′, and change the From box from Wall Top to Wall Baseline. Observe the results in the Floating Viewer. As you can see, you can move the wall modifier around the wall surface and resize it.

Pick the OK button to apply the settings to the wall. The results should look similar to Figure 5.29.

9. Save your file as EX5B.

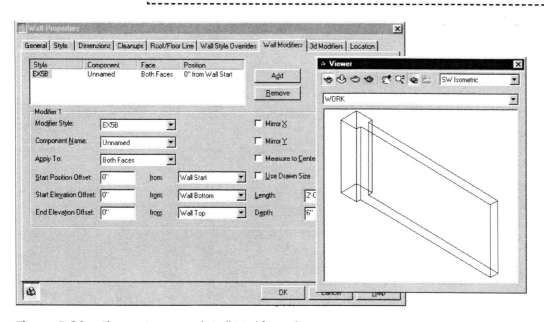

Figure 5.28   Floating Viewer and Wall Modifiers tab

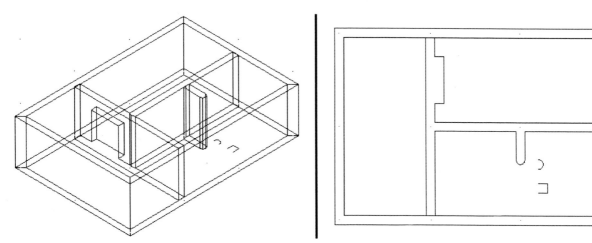

Figure 5.29   Results of new wall modifier style

Grids and Structural Members

You can add grids and structural members to your design. Grids are used to anchor objects to other objects, such as structural members like columns. You can anchor structural members to grids or place them freely in your design. Figure 5.30 shows the Grids and Structural Members toolbars.

Grids

There are two types of grids: column and ceiling. Both grids can be used to lay out objects, in a specified pattern, that are anchored to the grid. Ceiling grids can automatically be clipped to fit within a boundary.

To add a column grid, select the Add Column Grid tool. The Add Column Grid dialog box similar to Figure 5.31 appears. You can specify a rectangular or radial grid. Figure 5.32 illustrates the settings for a rectangular grid, and Figure 5.33 for a radial grid.

TIP: Creation Layer for Grids

If you're using the AIA layer standards set by the Desktop/Drawing Setup, the columns are created on the A-Grid layer and are blue.

Figure 5.30
(a) Grids and
(b) Structural Members
toolbars

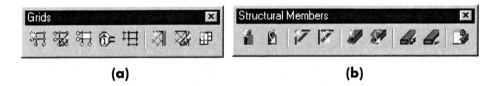

(a)   **(b)**

Figure 5.31   Add
Column Grid dialog box

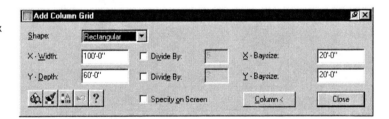

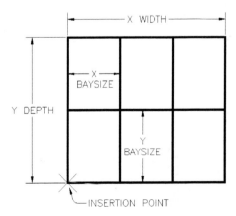

Figure 5.32   Rectangular grid

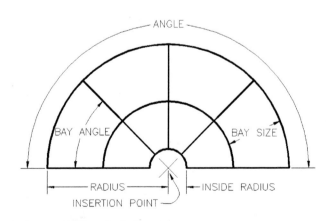

Figure 5.33   Radial grid

If you pick the Column button, you can pick the type of column that will be anchored to the intersection of the grid lines. To separate a column that has been anchored to a grid, pick the column and right-click to bring up the context menu. From the context menu, select Node Anchor/Release. You can also adjust the offset distances from the anchor point to shift the column.

The difference between a ceiling grid and a column grid is that the ceiling grid is automatically set to ceiling height and does not have a Column button. Instead, it has a Boundary button so that you can identify the boundary associated with the ceiling grid.

To modify a column grid, use the Modify Column Grid tool.

Structural Members

There are three types of structural members: columns, beams, and braces. Column objects are used to create vertical support members. Beam objects are used to create horizontal support members. Braces are used to create members that can be vertical, horizontal, or slanted.

To add a structural member select the appropriate Add tool, such as Add Column. The application is similar in all three cases. Figure 5.34(a) shows the Add Columns dialog boxes for each structural object type. Column objects are usually associated with a grid but you can place them freely if desired. Beams and braces can be placed anywhere in your design.

There are four structural styles preloaded but others are available when you open the member styles drawing. Figure 5.34(b) shows the Style Manager dialog box with the

TIP: Creation Layer for Structural Members

If you're using the AIA layer standards set by the Desktop/Drawing Setups, the structural members are created on the A-Cols layer, A-Beam layer, and the A-Cols-Brce layer, respectively, and are green.

Figure 5.34
(a) Add Columns and
(b) Style Manager
dialog boxes

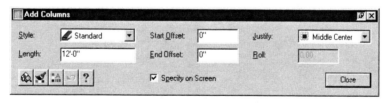

(a)

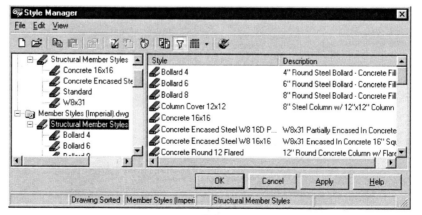

(b)

Structural Member Styles drawing open. The procedure to import styles was explained earlier in the section on wall styles.

You can create your own structural members from polylines by using the Convert tools for columns, beams, or braces. Basically the polyline profile defines the shape of the member, and it is extruded to create the three-dimensional form of the member.

Hands-On: Creating Grids and Columns

In this exercise, you'll create a column grid and place columns at the intersection points.

1. Open file iaadt3start, which is a blank file that contains all the necessary settings. Save it as EX5C.

2. Open the Work-3D tab and display the Grids toolbar.

3. Select the Add Column Grid tool. The Add Column Grid dialog box appears. Match your settings to Figure 5.35. Pick the Column button. From the Style drop-down list, select W8X31. This is a profile of a structure member 8 inches wide. Set the length to 15′ and pick the Close button to return to the Add Column Grid dialog box.

    Place the grid at 0,0 with a rotation of 0 degrees. Close the dialog box. Your screen should look similar to Figure 5.36. Observe how the columns are shown in 3D and 2D, depending on your view.

4. Save your file as EX5C.

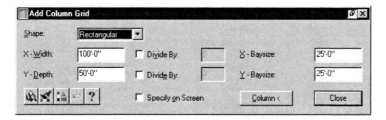

Figure 5.35   Add Column Grid dialog box

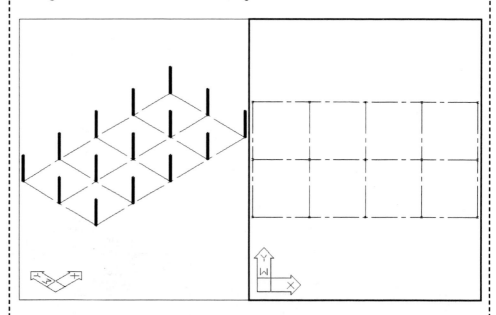

Figure 5.36   The column grid and columns in 2D and 3D

Roofs

There are two types of roofs: roof objects and roof slab objects. Roof objects are composed of the entire shape of the roof, including all sloped sides. These are used in the conceptual stage of the roof design. Roof slab objects are more complex and are composed of only one side of the roof. They are used in the design development stage. The first part of this section deals with roof objects that shall be referred to as roofs.

Roofs can be created with single or double slopes, with or without gable ends. They can be made from scratch or by using a polyline or a wall. The Roofs - Roof Slabs and Roof Slab Tools toolbars contain the necessary commands. Figure 5.37 shows the toolbars.

Creating a Roof

To create a roof, choose the Add Roof tool, or select Roofs/Add Roof from the Design menu. The Add Roof dialog box appears as shown in Figure 5.38.

The Shape drop-down list gives you two choices of roof: SingleSlope and Double-Slope. If you choose single, half the settings in the dialog box are grayed out.

From these settings you can add an overhang, create a gable end, and control the plate height, the rise, and the slope. The plate height is the height of the wall plate from the XY plane for a pitched timber roof. For flat concrete slabs, this is equivalent to the height of the wall at the intersection of the roof.

If you pick the Properties button, the Roof Properties dialog box appears. Selecting the Dimensions tab gives you access to the roof thickness. By default it's set to 10″ (see Figure 5.39). If you were modifying the properties of an existing roof, the upper boxes would be filled with roof data.

You can add an overhang, create a gable end, and control the plate height, the rise, and the slope.

TIP: Creation Layer for Roofs

If you're using the AIA layer standards set by the Desktop/Drawing Setup, roofs are created on the A-Roof layer and are orange.

Figure 5.37   Roofs - Roof Slabs and Roof Slab Tools toolbars

Figure 5.38   Add Roof dialog box

Figure 5.39   Roof
Properties with
Dimensions tab active

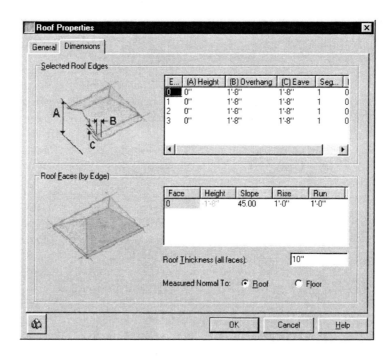

Drawing a Roof

Once you have filled in the appropriate boxes, you're ready to draw the roof. Basically, you pick the points around the perimeter of the wall. The roof is extended based on the overhang value.

You need to pick three points before you'll see the roof being constructed. You can pick as many points as you like to create any complex type of roof.

To create a gable roof, make sure the Gable box is not checked. Pick the two end points for the sloped portion of the roof, turn on the Gable box, pick the end point for the gable side, turn off the Gable box, pick the end point for the sloped side, turn the Gable box on, pick the viewport, and then press Enter. Remember that Gable cannot be selected for more that three consecutive edges.

Modifying a Roof

You can change any of the properties of a roof, such as plate height, rise, and slope. You can also edit edges and faces of the roof. To modify a roof, select the Modify Roof tool or select Roofs/Modify Roof from the Design menu. You'll be asked to select an existing roof. The Modify Roof dialog box is identical with the Add Roof dialog box, making it easy to make changes.

If you open the Properties dialog box, you can adjust the dimensions of individual components of the roof. Some values are not accessible, depending on the roof type. Figure 5.40 shows the Dimensions tab for a gable roof.

Converting Objects to a Roof

You can make use of existing walls or polylines to create a roof. If you select the Convert to Roof tool, you'll be asked to pick either walls or polylines to create a roof profile. Figure 5.41 shows the initial walls and the resulting roof.

Figure 5.40 Roof
Properties showing
Dimensions tab for a
gable roof

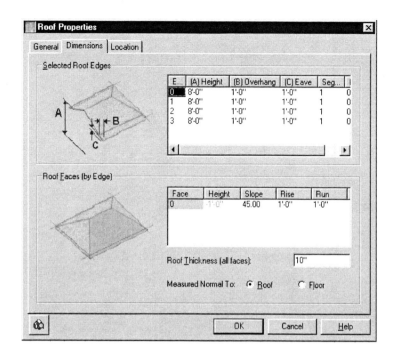

Figure 5.41
Creating a roof from
existing walls

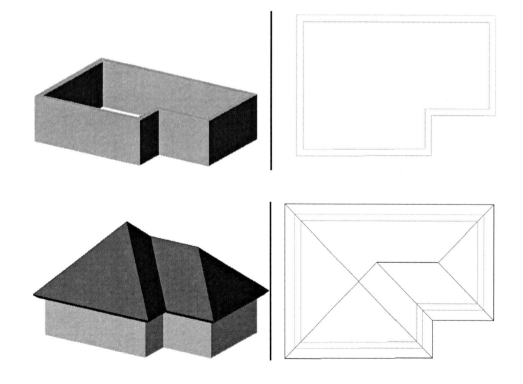

Hands-On: Creating a Roof

In this exercise you'll practice creating a roof and converting a series of walls to create a roof.

1.   Open file iaadt3start. Pick the Work-3D tab and display the Roofs - Roof Slabs toolbar. Save it as EX5D.

Drawing a Roof

2.   Select the Add Roof tool. Match your settings to those of Figure 5.42. Proceed with the following to create a roof with gable ends:

Make sure that the Gable box is not checked.

Pick point 0,0 for the start of the sloped side.

Pick point 40',0 for the end of the sloped side.

Check the Gable box so that it is on. You will need to pick inside the Top viewport to continue.

Pick point 40',20' as the end of the gabled side.

Make sure that the Gable box is not checked. You will need to pick inside the Top viewport to continue.

Pick point 0,20' for the end of the other sloped side.

Check the Gable box so that it is on. You will need to pick inside the top viewport to continue.

Press Enter to exit the command and close the dialog box.

The results should be similar to Figure 5.43.

3.   Save your file as EX5D.

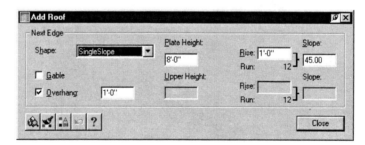

Figure 5.42   Add Roof dialog box

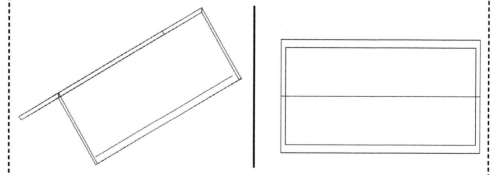

Figure 5.43   Creating a roof with gabled ends

Figure 5.44   Modify
Roof dialog box

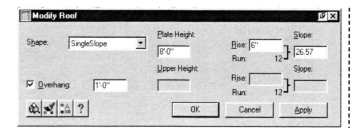

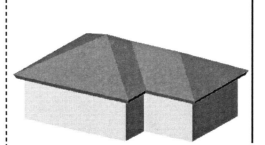
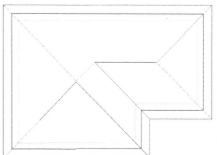

Figure 5.45   Creating a roof from four walls

Converting Walls to a Roof

4.   Open file adtex5E, which contains a series of walls. Save it as EX5E.

5.   Select the Convert to Roof tool and select all the walls. Enter NO when asked to erase layout geometry. The Modify Roof dialog box appears. Match your settings with Figure 5.44 and pick the Apply button. The results should look similar to Figure 5.45. Pick the OK button to exit the command.

6.   Save your file as EX5E.

Roof Slabs

A roof slab object represents a single side of a roof. Depending on its style it is composed of the roof, fascia, soffit, or frieze. Each slab is independent of the other and can be modified separately. You can trim, extend, and miter slabs, as well as cut holes or add and subtract mass elements.

Roof slabs are controlled by their styles. There are several styles preloaded into the startup drawing but you can load more by using the Roof Slabs Styles tool and opening the Roof Slab & Roof Slab Edge Styles drawing in the Style Manager. This procedure was explained earlier in the section on wall styles.

The easiest method to generate an entire roof using roof slabs is to create the concept initially using a roof object and then convert the roof object into individual roof slabs. This is accomplished using the Convert to Roof Slabs tool. Figure 5.46 shows elevation views of the edge of the roof and isometric views. Part (a) shows the roof object and part (b) shows the roof object converted to separate roof slabs.

Figure 5.46
Converting a roof object into separate roof slab objects

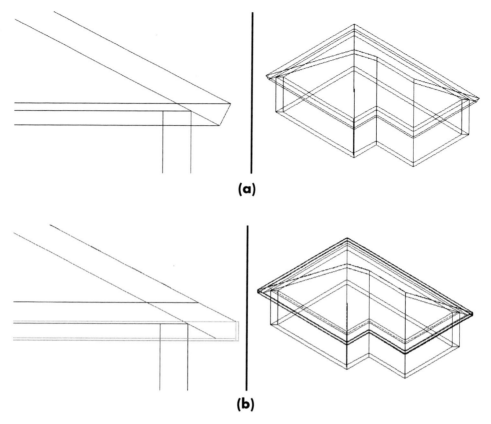

(a)

(b)

In a Nutshell

Adding walls, column grids, and sloped roofs is the first stage in refining your design.

Walls are complex intelligent objects that are easy to use. You can create walls using a wall style that controls their composition; automatic cleanup of intersecting walls makes their addition smooth.

Column grids allow you to add columns in a formatted layout. And to top it off, sloped roof construction is simple and straightforward.

The next step in the design development is the addition of openings, doors, and windows.

 ## Testing... testing... 1, 2, 3

Fill-in-the-Blanks

1. _____ are one of the most complex objects created in Architectural Desktop, but you may find them the easiest to manipulate because of their _____.

2. In the Add Walls dialog box, the _____ is used to apply automatic clean up of intersecting walls.

3. The cleanup radius determines _____

_____.

4. There are two types of grids: _____ and _____.

5. The Shape drop-down list gives you two choices of roof: _____ and _____.

Multiple Choice

6. The right-triangle icon that appears as you draw a wall
   a. stays at the start point of the wall.
   b. points toward the end of the wall.
   c. points toward the start of the wall as you draw.
   d. indicates the projected end of the wall, based on current information.

7. The appearance of the termination point on walls is determined by the
   a. wall style control.
   b. wall end style control.
   c. endcap termination control.
   d. wall endcaps control.

8. How many predefined member styles are preloaded in the startup drawing or AEC Arch (Imperial) drawing?
   a. four
   b. two
   c. six
   d. none

9. If you're using the AIA layer standards set by the Drawing Settings, the roofs are created on the A-Roof layer and are
   a. blue.
   b. orange.
   c. cyan.
   d. light green.

10. If you select the Standard wall style
    a. there is a 0 thickness to the wall.
    b. the wall has an automatic thickness of 1.
    c. you can enter any wall thickness you want.
    d. the wall thickness will have been preset.

 # What?

1. Briefly explain the three methods of creating walls.
2. Describe five modifications that you can make to already created walls.
3. What is one thing you cannot change about a newly created wall?
4. What's the purpose of a wall modifier style?
5. Explain the procedure, in detail, for adding a gable to a roof.
6. What is the difference between a ceiling grid and a column grid?

Let's Get Busy!

1. Create the floor plan shown in Figure 5.47 using wall commands. Do not dimension the plan. The outside walls are 6 inches thick and the inside walls are 4 inches thick; however, you can use whatever wall thickness you like. Some dimensions are missing, so you can estimate the wall locations.

2. Create the column grid shown in Figure 5.48. The X and Y values for the bays are 40 feet and 20 feet, respectively. The overall size is 80 feet in the X direction and 60 feet in the Y. As you create the grid use the custom shape column called W14X43, 15 feet high. You will have to copy the W14X43 structural member style from the Member Styles (Imperial) drawing using the Style Manager before you can use it for the grid.

3. Create the roof design shown in Figure 5.49(b). To start, draw a polyline as shown in Figure 5.49(a) and then convert it to a roof. The overhang should be 1 foot, the rise should be 4 feet.

Figure 5.47   Floor plan generated with wall commands

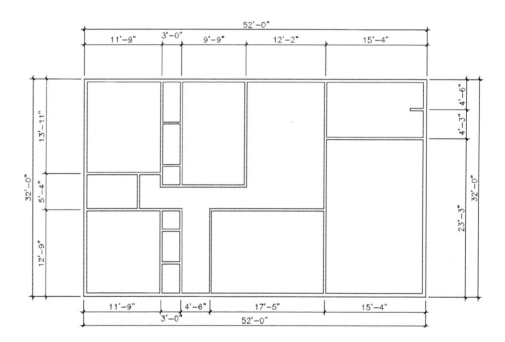

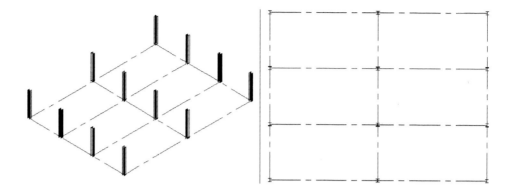

Figure 5.48
Column grid with
columns added

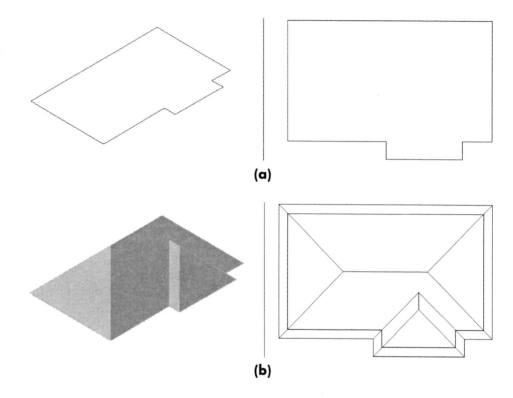

Figure 5.49   Roof
design

(a)

(b)

Chapter 6

Creating Openings

Ye Olde Trip to Jerusalem

Certainly the oldest pub in Nottingham, some say the oldest in Great Britain, this pub is built into the side of a rocky hill, with the castle of Nottingham looming directly above. At one time it was a brew house as well, and its chimneys go up into the rock and ultimately out of the hillside.

Key Concepts

- ◆ Doors
- ◆ Windows
- ◆ Openings

Creating Openings

The next stage in the design development is the application of openings. Openings can be classified as doors, windows, or simply openings, which are open spaces in walls. You can apply openings of any size, location, and elevation to a wall. There are custom door and window styles that can be sized for a variety of uses. Openings, doors, and windows are complete objects on their own but are designed to interact with walls and space boundaries. For the sake of simplicity, this chapter refers only to their application to walls.

You will find that the procedure to create and apply openings is very similar to that for doors and windows. To avoid repetition, common procedures for the applications for openings, doors, and windows will be explained only once. If necessary, the location of an explanation will be referenced for your ease.

The Doors - Windows - Openings toolbar contains most of the commands required to apply and modify openings. Figure 6.1 shows the toolbar.

You can apply openings of any size, location, and elevation.

Doors

Doors are usually placed in a wall; however, you can create freestanding doors as well, which, if you've been to a building supply store, isn't as unusual as you'd think. If the door is placed within a wall, it's constrained to the wall, meaning that it can't be moved outside the wall into open space.

Adding a Door

To create an opening, select the Add Door tool, or select Doors/Add a Door from the Design pull-down menu. An Add Doors dialog box similar to Figure 6.2(a) appears.

Figure 6.1   Doors - Windows - Openings toolbar

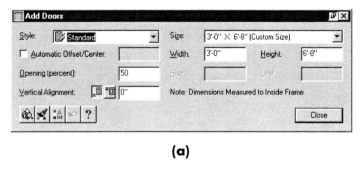

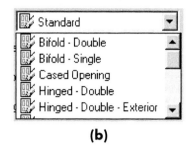

(a)   **(b)**

Figure 6.2   Add Doors dialog box and partial list of door styles

The Style drop-down list provides access to the door styles loaded into the drawing. Figure 6.2(b) shows a partial list. As with most other objects in Architectural Desktop, you can create your own custom doors. However, you'll find that there are plenty of door combinations already available to the beginner.

When you select the Standard door type, you can set it to any width or height you wish. If you select one of the predesigned doors, you can choose from a list of preset sizes, or you can set any custom size. The Opening (percent) box is used to adjust how much the door is open. You can also adjust vertical alignment so that windows and doors can easily be aligned with each other.

Figure 6.3 shows a single-hinged door displayed in the floating viewer. It can be helpful to open the floating viewer when choosing door styles. As you adjust the settings the door in the viewer changes. Once you're happy with the look, you can place it in your design.

To place the door, pick the wall on which you wish to locate the door. Make sure that OSNAP is turned off. As you drag the cursor, the door slides along the wall. If you move to an adjoining wall, the door follows. When the door is in the location you want, just press the pick button. Figure 6.4 shows a placed door.

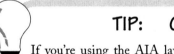

TIP: Creation Layer for Doors

If you're using the AIA layer standards set by the Desktop/Drawing Setup, the doors are created on the A-Door layer and are light blue.

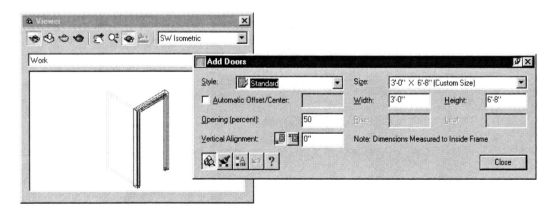

Figure 6.3   Single-hinged door shown in floating viewer

Figure 6.4   A placed
door

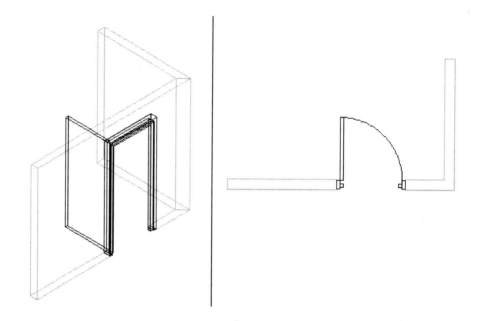

Accurately Placing a Door

Referring to the dialog box shown in Figure 6.2, note the Automatic Offset/Center box. If it is checked, you can enter a distance that the door will automatically be placed, away from the ends of walls or the center. As you drag the door into position, it automatically jumps to the proper location. You then just have to press the pick button to anchor the door in place.

Modifying a Door

To make changes to a door, select the Modify Door tool, pick the door to change, and press Enter. A Modify Doors dialog box similar to Figure 6.5 appears. It resembles the Add Doors dialog box, with similar settings.

To make more detailed changes, pick the Properties tool inside the Modify Doors dialog box. A Door Properties dialog box similar to Figure 6.6 appears. Using the Anchor tab, you can adjust the orientation of the door. This has the effect of changing the swing.

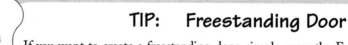

TIP: Freestanding Door

If you want to create a freestanding door, simply press the Enter key when asked to pick a wall. The door will then be free-floating, and you can place it anywhere in the design.

Figure 6.5   Modify
Doors dialog box

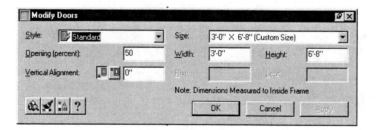

Figure 6.6   Door
Properties dialog box

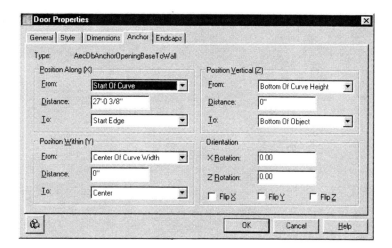

TIP: Moving a Door Along a Wall

You can move a door along a wall by selecting Doors/Repositioning Along Wall from the Design pull-down menu. You'll be asked to select the door. You can then pick the location for the door or use the Offset feature to specify the distance away from the point you pick.

You can also fine-tune the X, Y, and Z placement of the door. The Z placement has the effect of elevating the door within a wall.

Door Styles

As mentioned earlier, there are a number of predesigned doors from which you can choose. If you want to create your own door, copy an existing one, or load styles from another drawing, use the Door Styles tool to open the Style Manager dialog box (see Figure 6.7).

An easy way to make a new door is to copy an existing one and then make changes to the properties of the newly copied style. Once you have copied a style, highlight the name of the copy, right-click, and pick the Edit item from the context menu. A Door Style Properties dialog box similar to Figure 6.8 appears.

Figure 6.7   Style
Manager dialog box

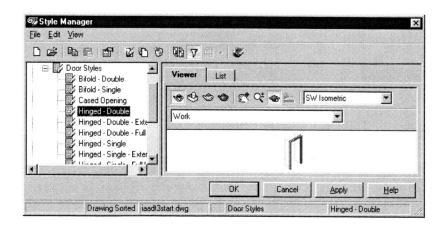

Figure 6.8 Door Style Properties dialog box

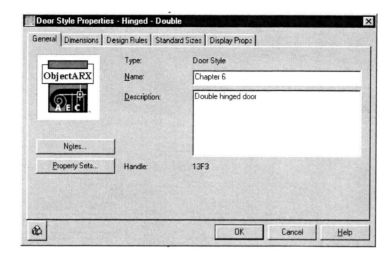

Figures 6.9(a)–(c) and the following text describe some of the various tabs. The Dimensions tab permits you to adjust the size of the frame, stop, and thickness, whereas the Design Rules tab permits you to adjust the shape of the door. You can create custom-shaped doors by creating AEC Profiles (explained in Chapter 3). The Standard Sizes tab permits you to create custom sizes, and the Display Props tab allows you to adjust how the door components are displayed. This adjustment is best left for when you're more experienced with using Architectural Desktop.

An easy way to make a new door is to copy an existing one and then make changes to the properties of the newly copied style.

Adding a Threshold

You can add a threshold to a plan view of a door very easily. Using the Display Props tab of the Door Style Properties dialog box, as shown in Figure 6.10, display Threshold Plan in the drop-down list and then pick the Edit Display Props button. The Entity Properties dialog box appears. Under the Layer/Color/Linetype tab you can turn on or off the display of the thresholds. Under the Other tab you'll find settings to control the size of the threshold. You may have to use the REGEN command to regenerate the drawing objects to see the threshold (see Figure 6.11). Remember, these settings affect all the doors that use this style. If you want to create a custom style, copy the existing style first and then make your changes. It is possible to add blocks to a door to customize it for 3D viewing; however, this is a more advanced topic and is not within the scope of this book.

TIP: Changing the Door Swing or Hinge Location

An easy way to change the swing or hinge of an existing door is to select Doors/Flip Swing or Doors/Flip Hinge from the Design pull-down menu.

Figure 6.9 Door Style Properties dialog box tabs

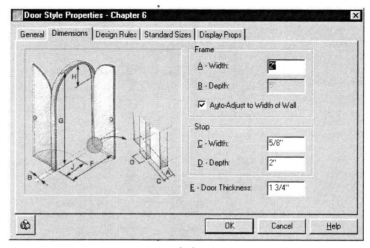

(a)

(b)

(c)

Figure 6.10   Display Props tab of the Door Style Properties dialog box

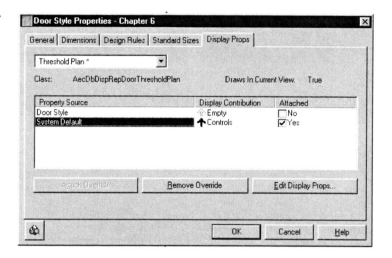

Figure 6.11   Entity Properties dialog box with the Other tab active

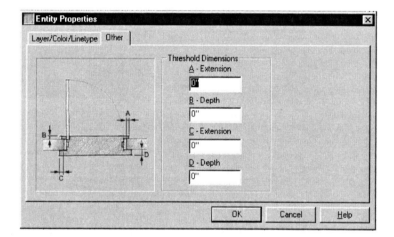

Hands-On: Adding Doors

In this exercise you'll add some doors and alter them after they have been placed.

1.   Open file adtex6A, which contains some simple walls that you can use to insert the different doors. Save it as EX6A.

2.   Display the Doors - Windows - Openings toolbar and activate the Work-3D layout.

Adding Doors

3.   Select the Add Door tool and match your settings to those of Figure 6.12. Pick an open area of the plan view and then press Enter. You'll notice that the door is free-floating. You'll be able to move the door anywhere in the design. This is how you create a freestanding door. Press the Esc key to abort the placement of the freestanding door.

Make sure OSNAP is turned off. Enter the Add Doors dialog box again and match your settings to those in Figure 6.12. This time pick a line that represents a wall in the plan view. Note how the door snaps to the wall.

Figure 6.12 Add Doors dialog box

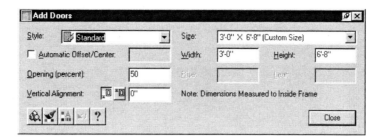

Figure 6.13 Placing the door in the approximate center of the wall

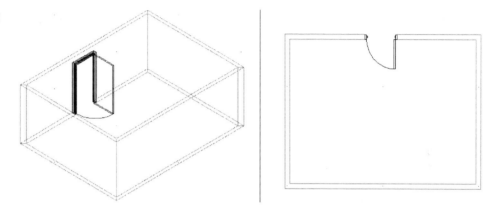

Drag your cursor around the plan, observing how the door moves around the plan but stays on the walls. Move your cursor inside and outside the plan and note how the swing switches from inside to outside. Place the door in the approximate center of the top wall as shown in Figure 6.13, and press Enter to exit the command.

Changing the Swing and the Hinge

4.   Select Doors/Flip Hinge from the Design pull-down menu, pick the door, and press Enter. The door hinge switched sides.

5.   Select Doors/Flip Swing from the Design pull-down menu, pick the door, and press Enter. The door's swing switched sides. Your door should now look similar to Figure 6.14.

Placing a Door Accurately

6.   Select the Add Door tool and match your settings to those of Figure 6.15. Note that the Automatic Offset/Center box is checked, and the value has been

Figure 6.14
Flipping the door hinge and swing

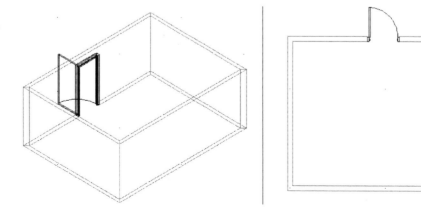

Figure 6.15 Add Doors dialog box with Automatic Offset/Center being used

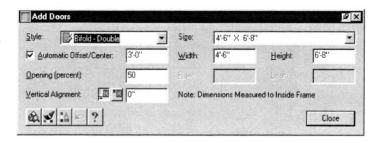

Figure 6.16
Accurately placing the door

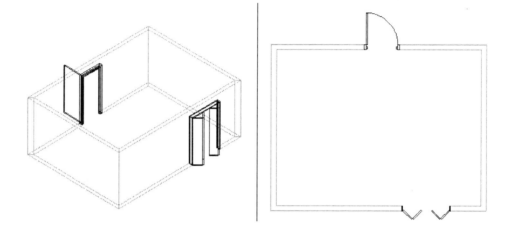

set to 3'. This will cause the door to automatically be set so that it is either 3 feet from the end of the nearest wall or from the nearest center depending on the placement of your cursor. Also note that you're going to place a Bifold-Double door this time.

Pick one of the wall lines and move the cursor. Note its behavior. Drag the cursor so that you're on the wall with the first door. The wall on each side of the existing door is considered a separate wall when you place a new door.

Place the door 3 feet from the right of the bottom wall by moving the cursor near the right end of the wall and picking. It automatically snaps 3 feet from the end. Press Enter to exit the command. Figure 6.16 shows the results.

7.   Erase the standard door on the top wall and see what happens. The wall is automatically reconverted to one continuous wall. Doesn't that make life easier?

8.   Save your file as EX6A.

Windows

An Architectural Desktop window object behaves in much the same way as a door object. The only difference is the objects that compose the window. You add and modify window objects in the same manner as door objects. Figure 6.17 shows the Add Windows dialog box.

As with the Add Doors dialog box, there is a setting for Vertical Alignment; this is usually set to match the height of the doors you'll use in your design. Also note the Rise box. It is active if you select a window that contains an arch or a peak. The rise sets the distance from the top of the peak down. The height is the overall height including the rise value.

Figure 6.18 shows two 4-foot-high windows, one with an arch, one without. You can see that they have the same overall height.

Figure 6.17   Add Windows dialog box

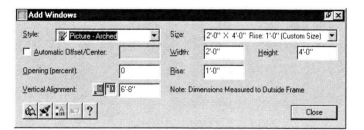

Figure 6.18 Window with and without arch

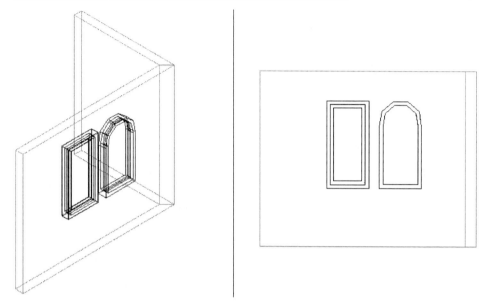

TIP: Creation Layer for Windows

If you're using the AIA layer standards set by the Desktop/Drawing Setup, the windows are created on the A-Glaz layer and are green.

You add and modify window objects in the same manner as door objects.

Adding a Sill to a Window

You can add a sill to a window in the plan view in the same way that you add a threshold to a door, as explained earlier. The only difference is that you work with the Sill Plan instead of the Threshold Plan.

Window Assemblies

A window assembly is a special type of object that provides a grid or framework for inserting objects such as windows and doors. With this framework, you can create complex window and door assemblies and insert them in standard walls, or use them as repeated elements in a curtain wall. This is an advanced topic and is explained in more detail in Appendix B.

Hands-On: Adding A Window

In this exercise you'll add a window to a wall and then make some adjustments.

1.   Open file adtex6B, which contains some simple walls that you can use to insert the different windows. Save it as EX6B.

2.   Display the Doors - Windows - Openings toolbar and activate the Work-3D layout. Make sure OSNAP is turned off.

Adding a Window

3.   Select the Add Window tool and match your settings to those of Figure 6.19. Pick a line that represents a wall in the plan view. Note that, like the door earlier, the window snaps to the wall.

Drag your cursor around the plan, observing how the window follows around the plan but stays on the walls. Using the Automatic Offset, place the window 2 feet in from the left of the bottom wall as shown in Figure 6.20, and press Enter to exit the command.

Modifying the Window

4.   You're now going to change the size and style of the window you just placed. Select the Modify Window tool, pick the window, and press Enter to continue. Match your settings to Figure 6.21 and pick the Apply button. The results should look similar to the design in Figure 6.21.

Figure 6.19   Add Windows dialog box

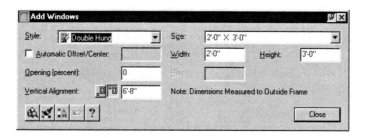

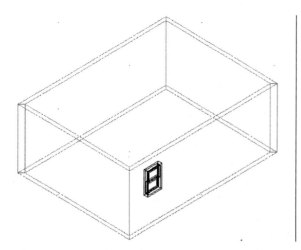
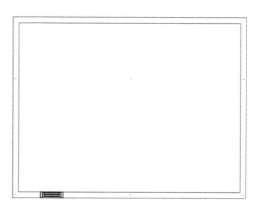

Figure 6.20   Placing the window 2 feet from the left of the bottom wall

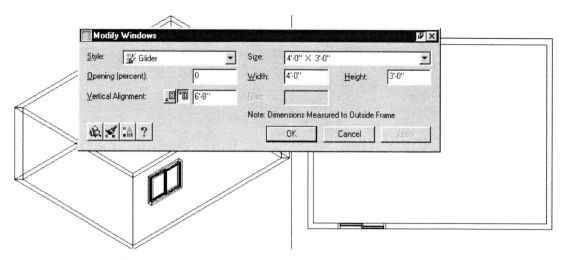

Figure 6.21   Modify Windows dialog box and modified design

As you can see, it's very easy to make changes to a window after it has been placed.

5. Save your files as EX6B.

Openings

You can create an opening of any size and elevation and apply it to a wall or even have it free-standing. You can apply predefined shapes or use custom shapes from existing AEC Profiles.

To add an opening, select the Add Opening tool. The Add Opening dialog box, similar to Figure 6.22, appears. Note that the settings are very similar to those of the Add Doors and Add Windows dialog boxes. The difference is the addition of a Custom Shape box and drop-down list. The application of the opening is the same as that for a door or window.

Figure 6.23 shows the placement of an arched opening. The 3D view has been shaded so that you can see the opening more clearly.

TIP: Creation Layer for Openings

If you're using the AIA layer standards set by the Desktop/Drawing Setup, the openings are created on the A-Wall-Open layer and are dark blue.

Figure 6.22   Add Opening dialog box

Figure 6.23
Placement of an
opening

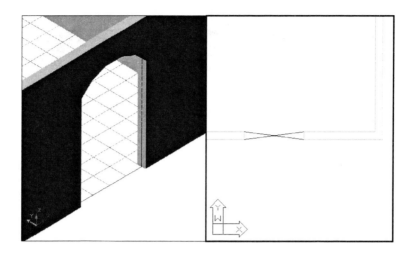

The Add Opening dialog box differs from the Add Doors
and Add Windows dialog boxes in the addition of a
Custom Shape box and drop-down list.

In a Nutshell

It's very easy to add openings to your walls or space boundaries. There are numerous pre-defined door, window, and opening styles from which to choose. You can also create your own custom openings using AEC profiles.

Because of the built-in intelligence of openings, you can anchor them to specific locations along a wall, allowing for semiautomatic placement. If you delete an opening, the wall is self-healing, making for efficient modifications.

You're now ready to start adding interior components, such as stairs and fixtures, to your design. This process is covered in the next chapter.

 Testing... testing... 1, 2, 3

Fill-in-the-Blanks

1. The three kinds of openings are

_____

_____

_____

2. The Dimensions tab permits you to adjust _____.

3. The Design Rules tab permits you to adjust _____.

4. The Standard Sizes tab permits you to create _____.

True or False

5. If you're using the AIA layer standards set by the Drawing Settings, the doors are created on the A-Door layer and are dark blue.   T or F

6. If the door is placed within a wall, it's constrained to the wall, meaning that it can't be moved outside the wall into open space.   T or F

7. If the Automatic Offset/Center box is not checked, you can enter a distance that the door will automatically be placed away from the ends of walls or the center.   T or F

8. Adding a threshhold affects all the doors that use the involved style.   T or F

What?

1. Outline the procedure for creating an opening in a wall.

2. Why is it useful to set a door an automatic value from a wall juncture or the center of a wall?

3. Why would you change the hinge side of a door? the degree of the swing?

4. How do you add a rise or a peak to a window?

5. What's the difference between a threshhold and a sill?

6. What could be the use of a freestanding door in an architectural drawing?

Let's Get Busy!

1. Open file adtex6C and add a standard door to the center of the wall as shown in Figure 6.24(a). Change the properties of the door so that it appears as shown in Figure 6.24(b). Save your file as EX6C.

2. Open file adtex6D and add a standard window (4′wide × 3′ high × 6′8″ head height) to the center of the wall as shown in Figure 6.25(a). Change the properties of the window so that it appears as shown in Figure 6.25(b). Save your file as EX6D.

3. Add windows and doors to the plan created in Chapter 5, Let's Get Busy!, Assignment 1. Figure 6.26 shows a possible layout.

Figure 6.24
Modifying a door's
properties

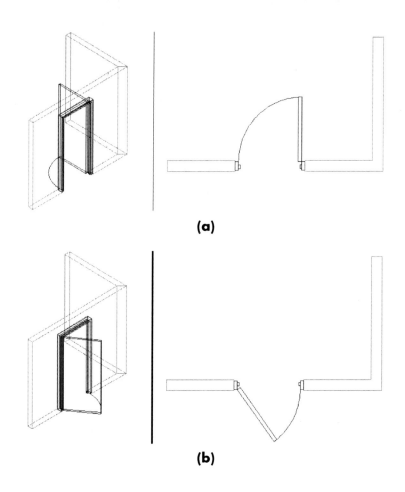

(a)

(b)

Figure 6.25
Modifying a window's
properties

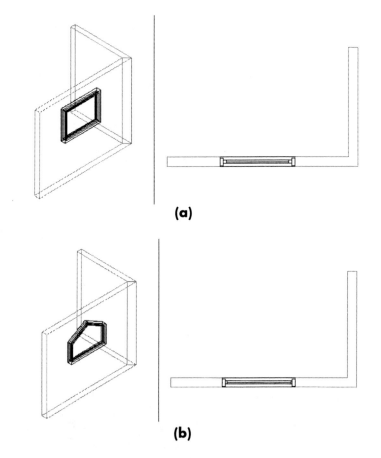

(a)

(b)

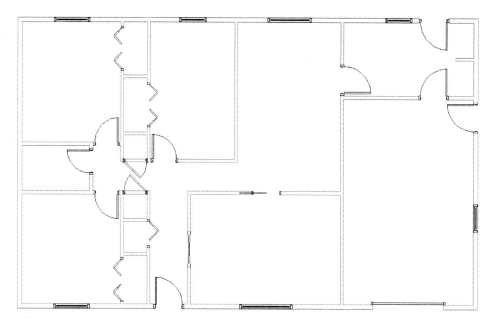

Figure 6.26 Adding windows and doors to a wall layout

Chapter 7

Interior Components

Stairstep Roof Outlines

This architectural detail is a holdover from the previous thatched roof period. This feature allowed either the homeowner or the thatcher to walk safely up the side of the roof to repair the thatching. Though thatch was replaced by slate, the style remains.

Key Concepts

◆ Stairs
◆ Railings
◆ Design Content

Interior Components

The final stage in design development covered in this text involves adding the interior components to the building, including stairs, railings, and design content. Design content comprises such items as appliances and furniture. Some of the content is in 3D, some in 2D.

This chapter explains the procedures for adding stairs and railings, and applying design content to your designs.

Stairs

You can create several types and shapes of stairs, complete with landings and turns. Some of the stairs are controlled by their length. Some lengths are constrained by the stair shape. The Stairs - Railings toolbar contains all the necessary tools (see Figure 7.1). Stairs can be added to the exterior of a building as well as to the interior.

Adding Stairs

The process of creating stairs is quite simple. When you select the Add Stair tool or select Stairs/Add Stair from the Design menu, an Add Stairs dialog box similar to Figure 7.2 appears.

You have your choice of seven different types: concrete, concrete ramp, standard, steel-open, steel-pan, wood-housed, or wood-saddled. Figure 7.3 illustrates some of the different types. The style can be open or closed, which refers to the condition of the rise opening under the tread.

TIP: Creation Layer for Stairs

If you're using the AIA layer standards set by the Desktop/Drawing Setup, the stairs are created on the A-Flor-Strs layer and are reddish brown.

Figure 7.1 Stairs - Railings toolbar

Figure 7.2 Add
Stairs dialog box

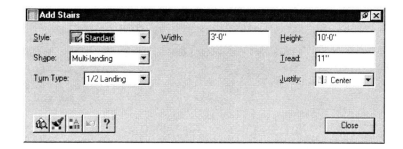

Figure 7.3 Types of
stairs

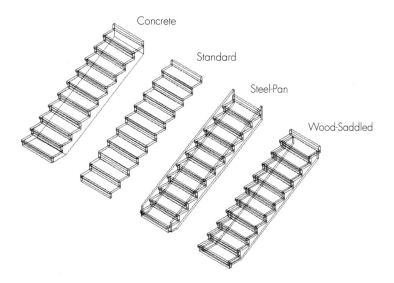

You also have your choice of four different shapes of stairs: multilanding, U-shaped, spiral, and straight. Figure 7.4 shows some of the different shapes.

The Turn Type section of the dialog box sets the landing turn for the next run of stairs and is controlled by the shape of the stairs. If you select multilanding stairs, you have access to all the types of next turns. If you choose U-shaped, the next turn is automatically set to half. The following is a description of the types of turns for landings:

Quarter Landing	Creates a flat landing where the stair run creates a right angle
Quarter Turn	Creates stairs where the stair run creates a right angle
Half Landing	Creates a flat landing where the stair run turns back in the opposite direction
Half Turn	Creates stairs where the stair run turns back in the opposite direction

Figure 7.4 Shapes
of stairs

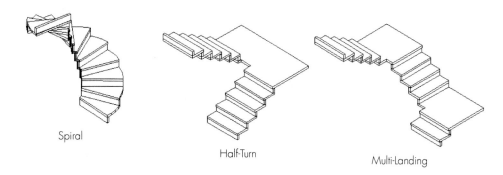

> *You have your choice of seven different types of stairs: concrete, concrete ramp, standard, steel-open, steel-pan, wood-housed, or wood-saddled.*

You can enter the total height of the stairs and their width. The tread, rise, and straight length are calculated for you. To adjust the design of the stairs, you can pick the Properties tool to display the Stairs Properties dialog box. This is explained later in this section.

Creating Multilanding Stairs

Once you've adjusted your settings, you're ready to start creating the stairs. First, pick the start of the bottom for the first flight of stairs. A long rectangle, attached to the cursor, is displayed (Figure 7.5(a)). This symbol would represent the total flight if the stairs were straight with no landings. The next stage is to pick a point where the first landing will be and then the length of the landing (Figure 7.5(b)). If at any time you pick a point beyond the length of the rectangle, it is assumed that you do not want any more landings, and the stairs are complete (Figure 7.5(c)). As you pick points to control the length, you also control the rotation of the stairs. Close the dialog box when finished. Figure 7.5(d) shows the results.

Creating U-Shaped Landing Stairs

After entering the settings in the dialog box, pick the start point for the bottom of the flight of stairs. A rectangle, attached to the cursor, is displayed (Figure 7.6(a)). This symbol represents two flights of stairs. As you drag the cursor, the width of the landing is created, as well as the rotation of the stairs. Pick a point to set the landing width and stair rotation. You can flip/mirror the position of the stairs by using the Horizontal buttons. This must be done before you finish creating the stairs. Close the dialog box when finished. Figure 7.6(b) shows the results.

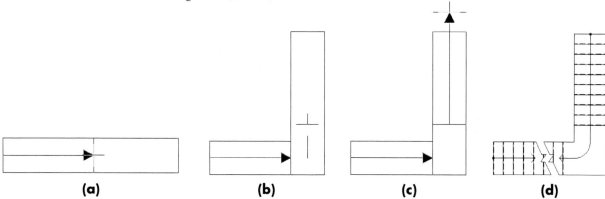

(a)   (b)   (c)   (d)

Figure 7.5   Creation of multilanding stairs

Figure 7.6   Creation of U-shaped stairs

(a)   (b)

Creating Spiral Stairs

Once you've entered your settings, pick the center of the spiral stairs, then pick a start point for the bottom of the flight of stairs. If the point is too close to the center, you'll see a red circle (Figure 7.7(a)). As you drag the cursor farther away from the center a curved section appears (Figure 7.7(b)). This curve represents the total flight of stairs. The farther away from the center, the larger the radius of curvature of the stairs. You can also rotate the stairs around the center as you locate the start point. Once you've established the start and rotation, you can then flip/mirror the position of the stairs. Close the dialog box when finished. Figure 7.7(c) shows the results.

Modifying Stairs

You can alter practically any property of a stair, such as height, width, and tread, from the Modify Stair dialog box. Select the Modify Stair tool, pick the stair, and press Enter to display the dialog box, as shown in Figure 7.8.

To adjust specific properties of the stair, pick the Properties tool to display the Stair Properties dialog box, as shown in Figure 7.9.

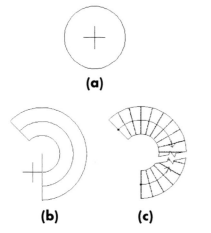

Figure 7.7   Creation of spiral stairs

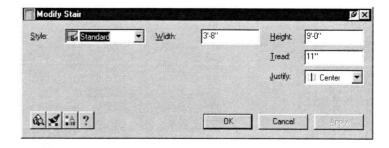

Figure 7.8   Modify Stair dialog box

Figure 7.9   Stair Properties dialog box with the Dimensions tab active

Figure 7.10   Stair Properties dialog box with the Constraints tab active

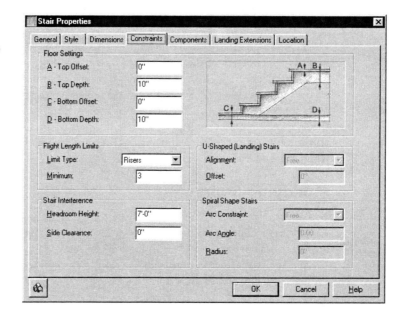

TIP: Adjusting Tread Size

If you want to adjust the tread size of a stair, you can make the adjustment after the stair has been created by using the Stair Properties dialog box. To access the dialog box, right-click on a stair and pick Stair Properties from the context menu.

With the Dimensions tab active, you can see that you can adjust individual components of the stair. Note the lock symbols. When the properties are locked, their values are calculated. The stair length is calculated by the tread size and riser count. If you lock the tread value, you can unlock other values, such as riser height, to make adjustments. The tread value, when locked, is calculated by the height of the stairs, number of treads, and the design rules. Design rules are minimum and maximum values that the treads and risers fall between when being calculated. This is set in the stair style. If you open the Constraints tab as shown in Figure 7.10, you can make adjustments to such things as floor settings and flight length limits. The Components and Landing Extensions tabs control values dependent on the stair style.

If you unlock the riser count or tread size and enter values that lie outside the values set under the Design Rules tab of the style you're using, an error message is displayed informing you of what is wrong. You should then alter the values so that they lie within the design rules.

You can alter practically any property of a stair, such as height, width, and tread, from the Modify Stair dialog box.

Stair Styles

Like most other objects in Architectural Desktop, stair objects can have different styles. You can edit, copy, and create new styles by accessing them through the Style Manager dialog box. Picking the Stair Styles tool displays a dialog box similar to Figure 7.11. Note

Figure 7.11   Style
Manager dialog box

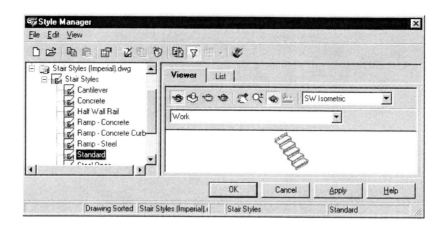

Figure 7.12   Stair
Styles - Standard dialog
box with the Components
tab active

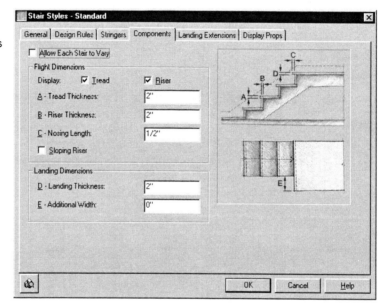

that the Stair Styles (Imperial) drawing has been opened. It contains several extra styles not contained in the template or startup drawing. You can drag stair styles from one open drawing to another. This is explained in Chapter 5 on wall styles.

If you highlight the style name and right-click, the context menu appears. Picking the Edit menu item brings up the Stair Styles edit dialog box as shown in Figure 7.12.

Under the Components tab, you have access to nosing data. The Stringers tab allows you to add stringers to the style. The stringer data are not available until you create the stringers. To create a stringer, pick the Add button and modify the stringer data.

The Design Rules tab allows you to set the rules from minimum, optimum, and maximum values for treads and risers.

Hands-On: Creating Stairs

In this exercise you'll create several stair types and modify their properties.

1.   Open file iaadt3start. Save it as EX7A.

2.   Pick the Work-3D layout tab and display the Stairs - Railings toolbar. Make sure the Ortho button is on.

Adding Multilanding Stairs

3.   Select the Add Stair tool and match your settings to those of Figure 7.13. Pick the Properties button to display the Stair Properties dialog box. Tab through the different sections without making any changes, just so you can see what has been calculated based on the stair height.

Under the Dimensions tab you should see a calculated length of 9'2". This means that the total length of the flights of stairs will equal 9'2". If you pick an initial length less that 9'2", a landing will be created. If you pick a location longer, you will get a single straight flight of stairs. The riser count is automatically calculated to be 11.

Under the Riser: you should see that the rise is calculated to be $6^{17}/_{32}$" and, by default, the tread is set to 11". *Note:* Lock the Tread lock symbol.

Pick OK to exit the dialog box and return to the Add Stairs dialog box. Set the start of the flight of stairs at 0,0 by picking or entering the coordinates. Now, pick beyond the 9'2" calculated length, along the positive X axis. A single length of stairs should be created. Use Zoom Extents in each viewport to see the stair object more clearly, as shown in Figure 7.14.

Modifying the Stairs

4.   Select the Modify Stair tool, pick the newly created stair object, and press Enter. The Modify Stair dialog box appears. In the Style drop-down box, pick Concrete, and then pick the Apply button to see the results. One after another, pick and apply each of the different styles so that you can see what they look like in the plan and 3D view.

Figure 7.13   Add Stairs dialog box

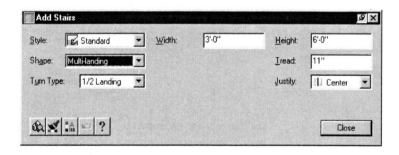

Figure 7.14
Closeup views of new stair object

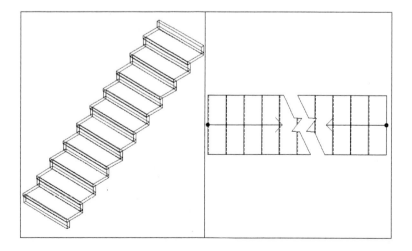

Figure 7.15 Add Stairs dialog box

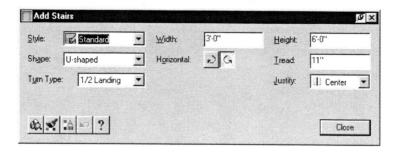

Figure 7.16 Closeup views of new stair object

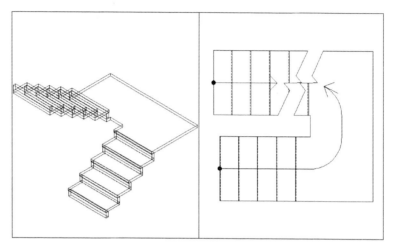

Creating U-Shaped Stairs

5. Erase the stair object you just created.

6. Select the Add Stair tool and match your settings to those of Figure 7.15. Note the Horizontal button is set to counterclockwise. Set the start of the flight of stairs at 0,0 by picking or entering the coordinates. Slide your cursor upward until it is 4 feet above the start point of 0,0. You should be able to see the outline of the stairs. The stair objects should now be created. Close the dialog box and use zoom extents in each viewport to the see the stair object as shown in Figure 7.16.

7. Save your file as EX7A.

Railings

As you might imagine, railing objects interact directly with stair objects, but you can have freestanding railings. Railings can be composed of a handrail, guardrail, posts, dynamic posts, balusters, and a bottom rail. Figure 7.17 shows the various railing components. *Note:* The dynamic posts are positioned based on the length of the railing. If the railing length changes, the dynamic posts reposition themselves.

TIP: Creation Layer for Railings

If you're using the AIA layer standards set by the Desktop/Drawing Setup, the railings are created on the A-Flor-Hral layer and are red.

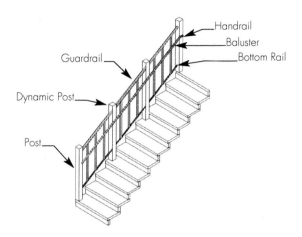

Figure 7.17   Railing components

Handrail
Baluster
Bottom Rail
Guardrail
Dynamic Post
Post

Adding a Railing

To add a railing, select the Add Railing tool, or select Railings/Add Railing from the Design menu. The Add Railing dialog box appears as shown in Figure 7.18. From this dialog box you have control over the style and placement of the railing. To access the specific design elements, you need to select the Style Manager for railings. This will be explained later in this section.

The positions of the handrail and the guardrail change depending on whether you use one or the other or both. If you use one or the other, it will be placed on top of the balusters and inside the posts. If you use both, the guardrail will be on top of the balusters, and the handrail will be lower and on one side or the other of the balusters.

The Attached To drop-down list is used to attach the railing object to a stair, stair flight, or to none (free floating). It's also possible to offset the stair railing.

The Automatic check box places the railing object automatically on the side of the stairs you pick, and creates it the entire length of the stairs. If Automatic Placement is turned off, you need to pick points to set the stair length.

Railing Properties

If you select the Properties button in the Add Railing dialog box, the Railing Properties dialog box appears. This dialog box displays information about the railings based on the selected style. However, you cannot modify the components or sizes. This is done by modifying the railing style as explained next.

TIP: Creation of Guardrails

Guardrails can be created on their own, without the other railing components. To create a new Railing Style, edit the new style by turning off all the other components under the Rail Locations tab.

Figure 7.18   Add Railing dialog box

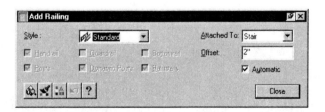

Railing Styles

The Railing Styles tool gives you access to the Style Manager for railings. The easiest way to make a new style is to copy an existing one. To copy an existing style, highlight the style, pick Copy from the Edit pull-down menu, and then pick Paste from the Edit pull-down menu. You can then rename the copied style.

If you edit a railing style, you can modify every component of the stair style. To edit a style, right-click on the style and pick the Edit button. You'll be presented with a dialog box similar to Figure 7.19.

Under the Rail Locations tab, you can turn on or off the various components and adjust their locations.

Under the Components tab, you specify the profile type and size. If you double-click on the profile name, a drop-down list appears as shown in Figure 7.20. You can then specify the shape of the component from the list of AEC profiles contained in the drawing.

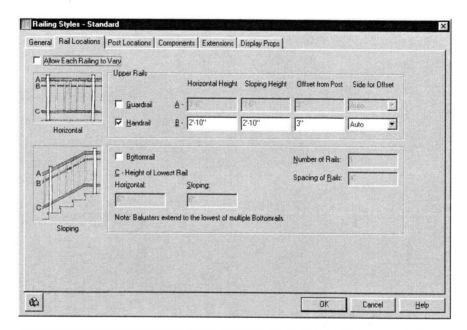

Figure 7.19 Railing Styles dialog box with the Rail Locations tab active

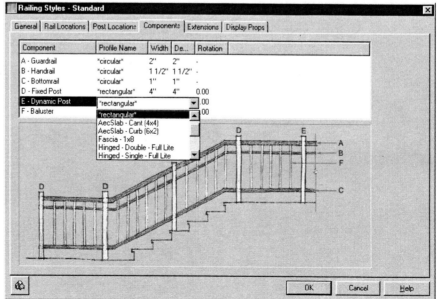

Figure 7.20 Railing Styles dialog box with the Components tab active

Figure 7.21   Modify
Railing dialog box

Figure 7.22   Railing
Properties dialog box
with the Anchor tab
active

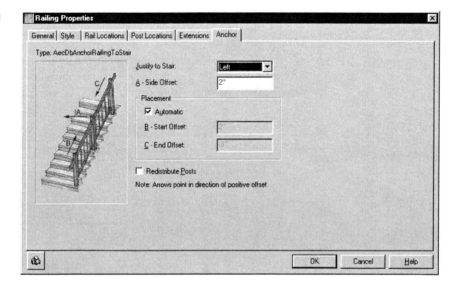

To create your own AEC profile, draw a closed polyline outline and select the Desk-top/Profiles/Profile Definitions pull-down menu item. You'll be presented with the Style Manager for profiles. Create a new profile style by right-clicking on the profile heading and picking New. To attach the polyline outline to the new style, right-click on the new profile name and pick Set From. Pick the polyline profile. You now have a new profile style to use for a railing component.

Modifying Railings

Using the Modify Railing tool, you can alter the railing style and offset and anchor prop-erties. A Modify Railing dialog box similar to Figure 7.21 appears.

If you pick the Properties tool in the Modify Railing dialog box, the Railing Proper-ties dialog box appears as before, but this time it has an additional Anchor tab as shown in Figure 7.22.

Hands-On: Adding Railings

In this exercise you'll add some railings to existing sets of stairs and then make some modifications to them.

1.   Open file adtex7B, which contains several different stair types. Save it as EX7B.

2.   Activate the Work-3D layout and display the Stairs - Railings toolbar.

Adding a Railing

3.   Zoom in on the straight flight of stairs marked A.

Figure 7.23 Add
Railing dialog box

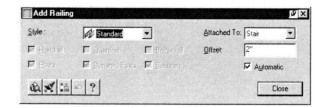

Figure 7.24 Railing
added to straight flight
of stairs

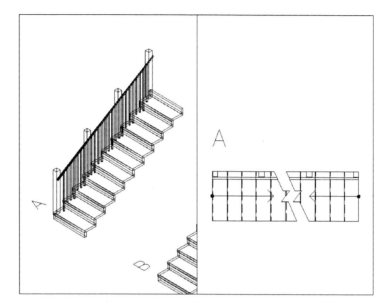

4.   Select the Add Railing tool and match your settings to those of Figure 7.23.
Pick the top side of the stairs in the plan view. The results should look like Figure 7.24.

Modifying a Railing

5.   Select the Modify Railing tool, pick the newly created railing, and press
Enter to display the Add Modify Railing dialog box.

Using the Style drop-down list, change the Standard style to the first style
in the list. Pick the Apply button to see the results. Repeat this, going through
each different railing style.

Adding a Railing to Multilanding Stairs

6.   Zoom in on the L-shaped stairs labeled B.

7.   Using the Add Stair tool, add a set of railings to the inside of the stairs as
shown in Figure 7.25. The railing should have only the guardrail and balusters.

8.   Modify the railing so that the anchor is placed on the opposite side of the
stairs. This is accomplished using the Properties tool on the Modify Railings
dialog box and opening the Anchor tab. Use the HIDE command to make the
results look like Figure 7.26.

9.   Zoom in on the U-shaped stair labeled C.

10.   Add a railing similar to Figure 7.27. The Attach To setting was set to Stair
Flight.

Figure 7.25 Adding a set of railings to multilanding stairs

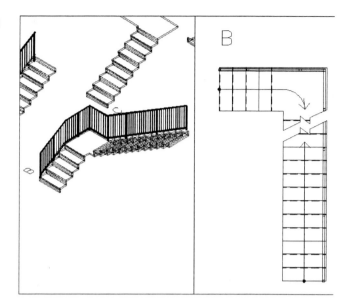

Figure 7.26 Changing the railing anchor

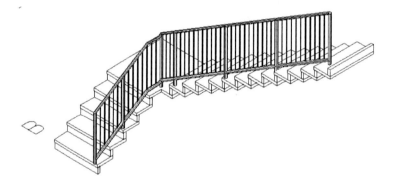

Figure 7.27 Adding a railing to the U-shaped stairs

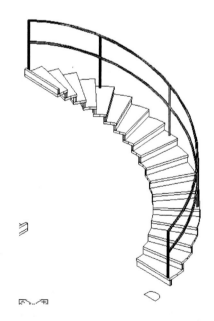

Figure 7.28 Adding a railing to the spiral stairs

11. Add a railing to the spiral stairs labeled D shown in Figure 7.28. The railing style was set to Guardrail - Pipe.

12. Save your file as EX7B.

Design Content

Design Content consists of various predrawn symbols that you can add to your design by simply dragging them from the DesignCenter window onto your drawing. Some of these symbols are in 2D; some are in 3D. There are two toolbars for accessing the design content: Design Content - Imperial and Design Content - Metric. Figure 7.29 shows the two toolbars.

Design Content consists of various predrawn symbols that you can add to your design by simply dragging them from the DesignCenter window onto your drawing.

The design content is accessed through the AutoCAD DesignCenter. The DesignCenter can be used to access existing drawings content. A description of the DesignCenter follows.

AutoCAD DesignCenter

The AutoCAD DesignCenter is a special window that allows you to browse through different sources of drawing content from existing drawings. The content can be in the form of blocks, dimension styles, layouts, linetypes, text styles, and Xrefs. You can drag the content from a drawing to the current drawing. Thus, you can create and store libraries of information in individual drawings and then drag the information into your current drawing as you require it.

You can access the DesignCenter from the Tools pull-down menu or the AutoCAD DesignCenter tool on the Standard toolbar. When you activate it, a window normally docked at the left of the screen appears, as shown in Figure 7.30.

Desktop and Open Drawings

You can view content contained on your computer's desktop or located in currently open drawings. The two tools are located at the left of the DesignCenter window. Picking the Desktop tool gives you access to any directory your system can access.

TIP: Creation Layer for Design Content

If you're using the AIA layer standards set by the Desktop/Drawing Setup, the Design Content objects are created on the layers associated with the symbol group. For instance, furniture is placed on the A-Furn layer.

Figure 7.29   Design Content toolbars

Figure 7.30
AutoCAD screen
showing DesignCenter

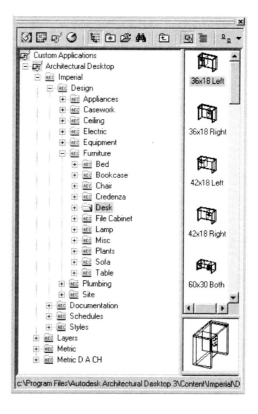

TIP: Scale of Design Content

The imperial and metric symbols are scaled for each type of unit of measurement. However, you can preset the units that blocks will use when they are inserted/dragged into the drawing. This is done within the Units dialog box.

The DesignCenter already has some drawings that contain symbols that you can use. These are normally located in the C:\Program Files\AutoCad Architectural 3\Sample\DesignCenter folder. By opening the directory tree you can access the various contents of any drawing file. To use the contents, pick the object in the content window that is to the right of the directory tree and drag it into the current drawing. The process is as simple as that.

When you use one of the Design Content tools, the DesignCenter automatically jumps to the correct folder for the imperial or metric symbols for Architectural Desktop.

Architectural Desktop Imperial Symbols

Symbol Group	Example
Appliances	ovens, dishwashers, washers, dryers
Casework	base cabinets, corner cabinets
Ceiling Fixtures	smoke detectors, ceiling fans
Electrical Fixtures	exit signs, fluorescent lights, incandescent lights
Equipment	elevators, office equipment
Furniture	sofas, chairs, desks
Plumbing	showers, baths
Site	signs, people, sports fields

Figure 7.31 View-dependent display of design content. (a) 3D view; (b) plan view; and (c) elevation view

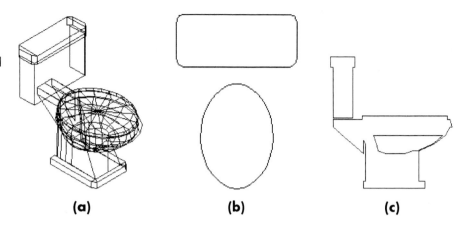

(a)   (b)   (c)

TIP: Changing the Design Content Menu

When you open the Content cascading menu from the Design pull-down menu, it contains either the Imperial or Metric Design Content. The choice is controlled by the AEC Content tab of the Options dialog box. You can access the Options dialog box from the Tools pull-down menu.

Architectural Desktop Metric Symbols

Symbol Group	Example
Bathroom Fittings	basins, baths, showers
Domestic Furniture	sofas, garden furniture, potted plants
Electrical Services	power outlets, switches
Kitchen Fittings	kitchen sinks, refrigerators
Office Equipment	conference tables, filing cabinets
Pipes and Ducts	pipe details, sanitary fittings
Site	street furniture, boats, trees

Viewing Design Content

Most of the symbols in the Design Content have been created so that they display differently depending on the display system active in a viewport. Figure 7.31 shows a single toilet object in a 3D view, plan view, and elevation view.

Hands-On: Using Design Content

In this exercise you'll practice applying Design Content by dragging content from one drawing to another.

1.   Open file adtex7C, which contains a simple design to which you can apply design content. Save it as EX7C.

2.   Activate the Work-3D layout, and display the Design Content - Imperial toolbar.

Adding Design Content from the DesignCenter

3.   Select the Furniture tool, and the DesignCenter window opens, displaying the folder for Furniture Design Content (see Figure 7.32).

Figure 7.32
DesignCenter displaying
folder for Furniture
Design Content

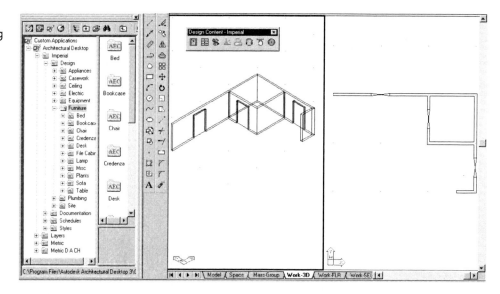

Figure 7.33   Chair
symbols and placed
Chair 2

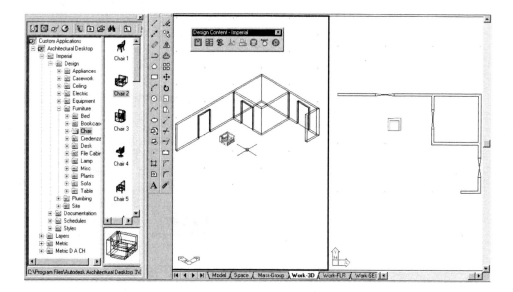

4.   Pick the Chair folder, and an image list of symbols appears to the right as shown in Figure 7.33. Pick Chair 2 in the image list to highlight it and drag it onto your design. After you place it you can move the cursor to rotate it into position. Match its position to Figure 7.33. The chair was placed on the A-Furn layer.

5.   Select the Plumbing Fixtures tool, and the DesignCenter switches to the Plumbing folder. Open the Bath folder and pick and drag Tub 30x42 onto your design, placing it in a position similar to that in Figure 7.34. The tub was placed on the A-Flor-PFix layer.

6.   Observe the symbols in the 3D view and in the plan view. Note that they're displayed differently, depending on the display system applied to the viewport.

7.   Save your file as EX7C.

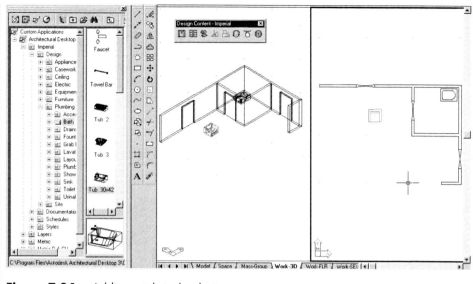

Figure 7.34   Adding a tub to the design

In a Nutshell

Adding stairs, railings, and design components is the final stage in the design development presented in this text. You can apply different types and shapes of stairs to your design, and you can modify the individual components that make up the stair object for practically any design requirement. This applies to the railing objects as well. You can apply railings to stairs or have them freestanding.

Design Content comprises predrawn 2D and 3D symbols that are view-dependent. To apply the Design Content objects, use AutoCAD DesignCenter to drag content from one drawing to another.

You've now gone through the basics of conceptual design and design development. The next step is to generate detail views of your design. This process is covered in the next chapter.

 # Testing... testing... 1, 2, 3

Fill-in-the-Blanks

1. List the seven stair types:

a. _____

b. _____

c. _____

d. _____

e. _____

f. _____

g. _____

2. When the properties are locked, their values are calculated. The stair length is calculated by _____ and _____.

3. Railings can be composed of:

a. _____

b. _____

c. _____

d. _____

e. _____

f. _____

4. The AutoCAD DesignCenter is a(n) _____ that allows you to browse through different sources of drawing content from existing drawings.

What?

1. What is the difference between open and closed stairs?

2. List and describe the four shapes of stairs.

3. Explain the four types of turns for stairs. What limitations are there on the types of stairs with which these turns will work?

4. What happens if you unlock the riser count or tread size and enter values that lie outside the design rules?

5. Name and give an example of five symbol groups in Imperial and five in Metric for Architectural Desktop.

6. What color are the Design Content elements when drawn on their layer?

Let's Get Busy!

1. Create the various stair layouts shown in Figure 7.35. Save your file as EX7D.

2. Add railings to the stair layouts as shown in Figure 7.36. Save your file as EX7D.

3. Add interior components to the plan updated in Chapter 6, Assignment 3. Figure 7.37 shows a possible layout. Save your file as EX7E.

Figure 7.35 Stair
layouts

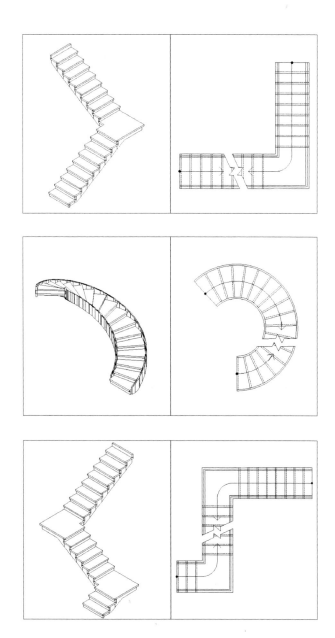

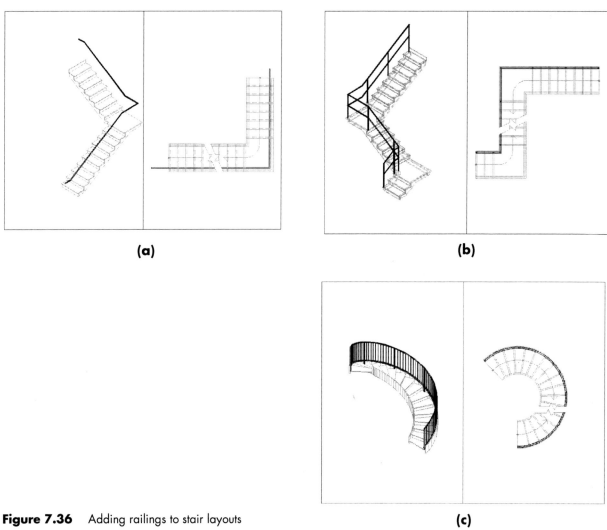

Figure 7.36 Adding railings to stair layouts

(a)

(b)

(c)

Figure 7.37 Adding
interior content to a
floor plan

Chapter 8
Representation Views

Thatched Roof

This thatched roof on the Culloden battlefield's small hospital shows a method that was used for holding down straw and mud thatch. Look closely to see ropes and the weighty tree branches and stones that hung over the thatching. Roofing architecture has changed a great deal since this period!

Key Concepts

- ◆ Elevations
- ◆ Sections
- ◆ Perspectives

Representations

Up to this point you've been using plan, isometric, and orthographic views to present your design. This chapter explains the methods necessary to generate elevation, section, and perspective views. With elevation and section views you can specify what parts of the design will be presented. Perspective views make use of a camera to display the desired view similar to the way the human eye sees, allowing you to show a more realistic view of your design.

All three types of representations discussed in this chapter make use of a three-dimensional model.

Elevations

In Architectural Desktop an *elevation* is an object derived from an elevation line and existing objects in your design. You can update the elevation object if the design of the building changes, and you can create an elevation of any part of the building, including and excluding objects as you desire.

The elevation object is basically a duplication of the model. The difference lies in the inclusion or exclusion of objects, so that you can make the elevation as simple or as detailed as you want. The other difference is that you can define the depth of the elevation view, thereby excluding background objects.

A quick method of creating the four common elevation views (front, rear, right side, and left side) is to create one elevation object that includes all the exterior objects. Then you can create four different viewports that contain the four elevation views. Figure 8.1 shows the Elevations and Sections toolbars. You'll notice that the toolbars contain very similar tools. The creation of an elevation or a section is almost the same.

Creating an Elevation Line and Mark

The first step in creating an elevation object is to create an elevation line and mark. The *elevation line* defines the area to be included in the elevation object. The *mark* is an indicator, telling you the direction in which the elevation line was created. This feature is useful when you want to clip out background objects.

Figure 8.1 Elevations and Sections toolbars

2221222

22222222222

TIP: Creation Layer for Elevation Line and Mark

If you're using the AIA layer standards set by the Desktop/Drawing Setup, the elevation line and mark are created on the A-Sect-Iden layer and are greenish blue.

To create the elevation line and mark, select the Add Elevation Line tool. You will be asked to define the start and end of the elevation line, which defines the orientation and size of the viewing plane of the elevation. For standard elevation views it's a good idea to turn ORTHO on so that your elevation line is aligned with an axis. Also, the elevation line should extend past the objects you want to include in the elevation object. Figure 8.2 shows the elevation line in the plan and 3D views. In both the plan view and the 3D view, the elevation line is shown as a rectangular box defining the area of the elevation view.

You can use grips to adjust the elevation line's position, length, and area.

> The elevation object is basically a duplication of the model. The difference lies in the inclusion or exclusion of objects, so that you can make the elevation as simple or as detailed as you want.

Creating an Elevation Object

To create an elevation object from an elevation line, select the Create Elevation tool. You will be asked to select the elevation line. The Generate Section/Elevation dialog box then appears, as shown in Figure 8.3. The choice made here controls whether you generate a 3D or 2D elevation, what objects you want to include in the elevation, where you want to place the elevation object, and the type of display when the elevation is placed in the drawing. The 3D button generates a three-dimensional elevation object and the 2D button generates a two-dimensional elevation object. The display set controls what objects are displayed in the viewport. For example, the Plan display representation set displays

Figure 8.2 Elevation line and marker in (a) 3D and (b) 2D views

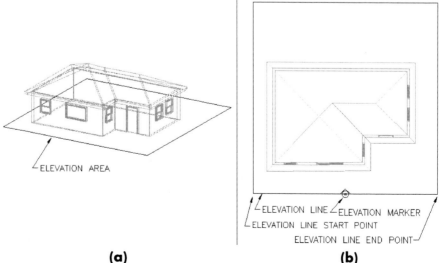

(a)　　　　(b)

Figure 8.3
Generate
Section/Elevation
dialog box

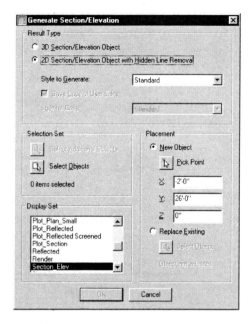

TIP: Creation Layer for Elevation Object

If you're using the AIA layer standards set by the Desktop/Drawing Setup, the elevation object is created on the A-Elev layer and is blue.

the 2D plan version of the objects, and the Model Style displays the elevation in 3D. We suggest you use the Section_Elev display representation.

You need to use the Select Objects button to pick what parts of the model you want included in the elevation object.

Under Placement you'll notice New Object and Replace Existing buttons. Use New if this is the first time the elevation object is being created. Use Existing if you want to add to an existing elevation object. *Note:* If you're adding to an existing object, you must select the previous objects as well as the new objects to be included in the elevation.

Finally, you need to use the Pick Point button for the displacement. This is to situate the new elevation object. You can place it, superimposed, over the model or move it to a new location. It is often useful to place the elevation object a distance away from the original model so that it won't interfere in the various viewport configurations.

The elevation object then appears, showing only the objects you selected. Using the elevation object, you can create a viewport layout to contain only the elevation views.

Pick the OK button to generate the elevation.

Creating a Layout for Viewing the Elevation Object

To create a new layout, right-click on the tab of an existing layout, and pick New Layout from the context menu. Go through the typical procedure to create the layout, such as specifying the plotting setup, and give it the name Elevation. A viewport is already created. Erase it and create your own viewports. Activate each one in turn and assign the Plot Viewport Display Configuration by selecting Select Display from the Desktop pull-down menu. The elevation objects are visible only when you display an elevation view such as front or right in the viewport.

You may need to freeze the other objects so that only the elevation object is visible. You'll also want to assign the Hideplot option to the viewport so that when you plot the

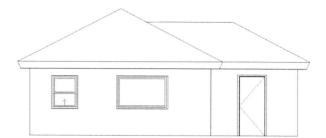

Figure 8.4 Elevation view of elevation object

TIP: Objects Included in an Elevation

When an elevation object is created, only those objects whose layers are on (not frozen) will be included. Even the Update feature won't add objects on previously frozen or turned-off layers. However, you can create the elevation again to include all the required objects.

viewport you see only the exterior of the elevation object. You can assign the Hideplot option to the viewport by using the PROPERTIES command or the MVIEW command.

You'll notice that door swings and window opening indicators have been added to the view (see Figure 8.4).

Updating an Existing Elevation

If you make changes to your original model, you can update an existing elevation by selecting the Update Elevation tool. You are then asked to pick the elevation object to update. It changes to reflect any modifications to the model. If you added objects to the model, you'll need to add them to the elevation by using the Create Elevation tool again.

Hands-On: Creating an Elevation Object

In this exercise you'll create an elevation line and marker and use them to create an elevation object.

1.   Open file adtex8A, which contains a simple model of a house that you will use to create the elevation objects. Save it as EX8A.

2.   Activate the Work_3D layout tab and display the Elevations toolbar. Turn ORTHO on.

Creating an Elevation Line and Marker

3.   Activate the Plan viewport and select the Add Elevation Line tool. See Figure 8.5 for the location of the start and end points of the elevation line. The elevation line should appear as shown in Figure 8.5. Note the rectangle in the 3D viewport that shows you the extents of the elevation line.

Creating the Elevation Object

4.   Select the Create Elevation tool and pick the elevation line you just created. The Generate Section/Elevation dialog box appears. Set the Result Type to 3D and

Figure 8.5 (a)
Creation of elevation
line and (b) marker

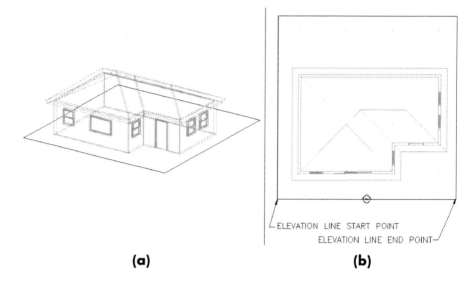

ELEVATION LINE START POINT
ELEVATION LINE END POINT

(a)   **(b)**

pick the Select Objects button. Select all the objects that represent the building. If this were a more complex building, you could exclude the interior objects.

Make sure the New Object button is selected and use the Pick Point button to identify where the elevation object will be placed. Pick a point above the model similar to Figure 8.6.

Check that the Display Set is set to Section_Elev and select the OK button.

Use Zoom Extents in both viewports. The results should look similar to Figure 8.6. The elevation object is a duplicate of the objects you picked from the original model. If you zoom in on the windows and doors of the elevation object, you'll notice the addition of door swings and opening directions.

Creating the Elevation View

5.   Pick the Template-Overview layout tab (you may have to scroll to see it). You should see the top and bottom viewports showing a front and side elevation

Figure 8.6 Creation
of elevation objects

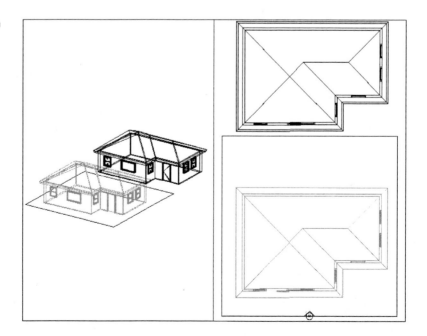

view of the model and the elevation object. These can be used to view and print your elevation or section views.

6.   You're going to create a new layout specifically for the elevation views. Right-click on the Template-Overview tab and select New Layout from the context menu. A new layout tab appears next to the Template-Overview tab.

Right-click on the new layout tab and select Rename from the context menu. In the dialog box, enter Elevations for the layout name.

Pick the Elevations tab. The Page Setup dialog box may appear. Enter your settings as you would for a plot and OK the dialog box. The new layout appears with a floating viewport already created.

Erase the viewport and create two new viewports that are side by side on a new layer called VPORTS. Use the MVIEW command to create the viewports. They should be similar to Figure 8.7.

7.   Freeze the layers for the objects in the model. In this case, the layers are A-Door, A-Glaz, A-Roof, and A-Wall. Only the elevation object should be visible. You may need to freeze layers A-Door, A-Glaz, A-Roof, and A-Wall to see the elevations properly.

8.   Switch to model space, either by typing MS or picking the Paper button, turning it to Model.

9.   Activate the left viewport and pick Select Display from the Desktop pull-down menu. From the Viewport Display Configuration dialog box, highlight Plot and pick the OK button. The plan view should have disappeared in the left viewport. This is because the elevation object can be seen only when an elevation view is displayed.

10.   Display the front view in the left viewport using the Front View tool. The front elevation is now displayed.

11.   Repeating Steps 9 and 10, display the Right View in the right viewport.

12.   Use the HIDE command in each viewport to show only the exterior of the elevations. The results should be similar to Figure 8.8. Note that the scales do not match in each viewport. Use the Zoom option to match the viewports if desired. If you used a specific paper size and know what the plot scale would be, try to use the XP option of the ZOOM command, such as ZOOM 1/48 XP.

13.   To set the viewport to plot with hidden line removal, you need to use the MVIEW command again. Switch to paper space again and enter the MVIEW

Figure 8.7   Two new viewports

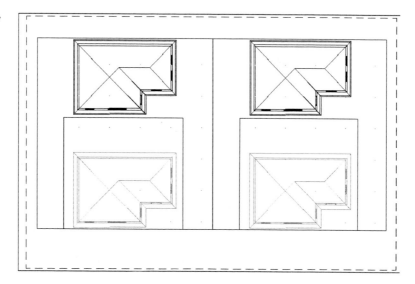

Figure 8.8
Viewports showing front and right elevation views, hidden

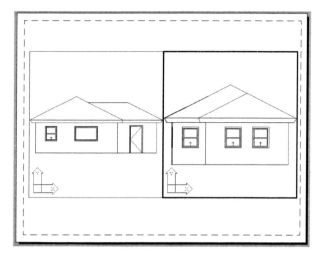

command. Enter Hideplot as the option, enter ON, and pick both viewports. When you plot the Elevations layout, both viewports plot with hidden lines removed.

Updating the Elevation Object and Views

14.   Activate the Work-3D tab and thaw the A-Glaz, A-Door, A-Roof, and A-Wall layers.

15.   Using the Modify Window tool, pick the double-hung window on the far left. Change it to a Picture-Arched window.

16.   Select the Update Elevation tool and pick the elevation object. The Generate Section/Elevation dialog box appears. Pick the OK button. Note how the elevation object changed to reflect the modified window.

17.   Switch to your Elevations layout tab and see the results. The window has changed there as well.

18.   Save your file as EX8A.

Sections

In Architectural Desktop a section is an object derived from a section line and existing objects in your design. The process for creating a section object is identical with that for creating an elevation object. The difference is that you can create a section line that can be stepped, instead of just a straight elevation line.

Creating a Section Line and Mark

The procedure for creating section lines is the same as for creating an elevation line. The difference is that you draw the line where you want to section the model. The line also can have as many steps as necessary to allow you to cut into various areas of the model. Like the elevation line, the section line has a length distance and a height distance. These distances establish the 3D section box from which the section object is created.

To create the section line and mark, select the Add Section Line tool. You will be asked to define a section polyline. It has a start and end as well as step points. To create a straight section use no step points. The section polyline defines the orientation and size of the viewing plane of the section. Figure 8.9 shows the section line in the plan and 3D views. In the plan view it's displayed as a closed polyline. In the 3D view it's shown as a volume.

Figure 8.9 Section
line and marker in (a)
3D and (b) 2D views

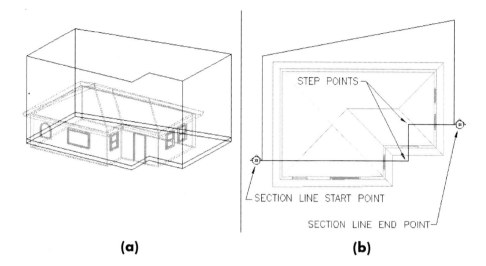

(a)   **(b)**

TIP: Creation Layer for Section Line and Mark

If you're using the AIA layer standards set by the Desktop/Drawing Setup, the
elevation line and mark are created on the A-Sect-Iden layer and are brown.

**The line can have as many steps as necessary to
allow you to cut into various areas of the model.**

You can use grips to adjust the section line's position, length, and volume.

Creating a Section Object

To create a section object from a section line, select the Create Section tool. You'll then be
asked to select the section line; the Generate Section/Elevation dialog box appears.

The procedure to generate the section object is the same as that for an elevation
object. Once you've made your settings and picked the OK button, the section object then
appears, showing only the objects you selected. Figure 8.10 shows the created section
object in the plan and 3D viewports. Using the section object you can create a viewport
layout to contain only the section views.

TIP: Creation Layer for Section Object

If you're using the AIA layer standards set by the Desktop/Drawing Setup, the section object is created on the A-Sect layer and is brown. The edges of the section portion of the section object are created on the A-Sect layer and are reddish.

Figure 8.10   Section
object

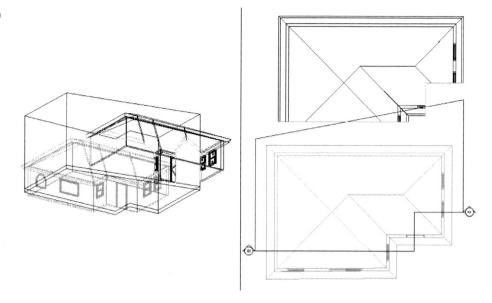

Figure 8.11   Section
view of a section object

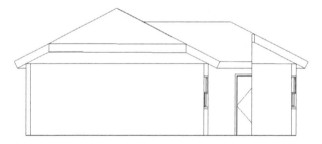

Creating a Layout for Viewing the Section Object

To create a new layout to display the section object, follow the procedure outlined for creating a layout for an elevation object.

Figure 8.11 shows a section view.

Updating an Existing Section

If you make changes to your original model, you can update an existing section object by selecting the Update Section tool.

Hands-On: Creating a Section Object

In this exercise you'll create a section line and marker and use these to create a section object.

1.   Open file adtex8B, which contains a simple model of a house that you will use to create the section objects. Save it as EX8B.

2.   Activate the Work_3D layout tab and display the Sections toolbar. Turn ORTHO on.

Creating the Section Line and Marker

3.   Activate the Plan viewport and select the Add Section Line tool. Refer to Figure 8.12 for the location of the start and end points of the section line. Use the default length and height of 20 feet. The section line should appear as shown in Figure 8.12. Note the box in the 3D viewport that shows you the extents of the section line.

Creating the Section Object

4.   Select the Create Section tool and pick the section line you just created. Next, select all the objects that represent the building. If this was a more complex building, you could exclude the interior objects.

The Generate Section/Elevation dialog appears. Set the Result Type to 3D and pick the Select Objects button. Select all the objects that represent the building. Make sure the New Object button is selected and use the Pick Point button to identify where the elevation object will be placed. Pick a point above the model similar to Figure 8.13. Check that the Display Set is set to Section_Elev and select the OK button.

Figure 8.12
Creation of section line and marker

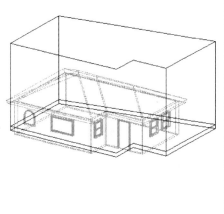
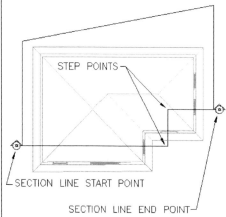

Figure 8.13
Creation of section objects

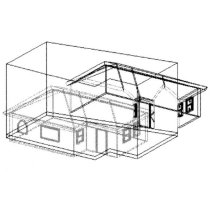
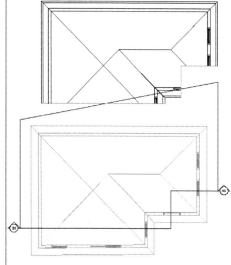

Use Zoom Extents in both viewports. The results should look similar to Figure 8.13. The section object is a duplicate of the objects you picked from the original model. If you zoom in on the right end-walls of the section object, you will notice the details of the windows that were sectioned.

Creating the Section View

5.   Create a section layout to contain the two section views: front and right. Follow the same procedure you used to create the elevation layout.

6.   Save your file as EX8B.

Perspectives

In Architectural Desktop, perspectives are derived from the placement of a camera object. The camera is modeled after real-world cameras, making use of through-the-lens viewing.

The benefit of the camera object is that it's easily adjusted with grips, and you can have more than one camera object in your model, which allows you to switch to any camera view at any time. Finally, you can use a camera to create an animated sequence to allow model viewing in motion.

The tools used to manipulate a camera are contained in the Perspectives toolbar as shown in Figure 8.14.

Adding a Camera

Normally, it's easier to add a camera to a plan view. To add a camera to your model, select the Add Camera tool, and the Add Camera dialog box appears as shown in Figure 8.15.

It's important to give the camera a name so that you can keep track of it when you want to switch from one camera view to another.

The Zoom box is used to enter the lens size. A value of 50 represents a 50-mm lens. This is close to what the unaided human eye sees. A value above 50 is considered a telephoto lens, used for closeup views of faraway objects, and less than 50 is considered a wide-angle lens, used to widen the field of view (FOV), allowing you to see more of the scene.

The Eye Level box is used to enter the height location of the camera initially. You can adjust this value later.

The Generate View After Add box allows you to apply the camera view to a selected viewport after you have placed the camera.

The Viewport Association box is used to associate a camera with a particular viewport. This is used to control the orientation of the camera and therefore the resulting view.

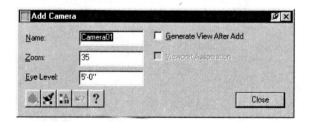

Figure 8.14   Perspectives toolbar   **Figure 8.15**   Add Camera dialog box

> **The benefit of the camera object is that it's easily adjusted with grips, and you can have more than one camera object in your model, which allows you to switch to any camera view at any time.**

Once you have made your settings you can place the camera using the insertion point. You'll then be asked to locate the target point. This is the center of interest for your perspective view. Drag the cursor and pick a point, or enter the coordinates. As you drag the cursor you'll see a cone that represents the FOV for the lens you entered. This cone shows what area will be covered with the lens you chose. You can modify this at any time after you place the camera object. Figure 8.16 shows the sequence for adding a camera.

Once the camera is added, you can apply its properties to a viewport to generate the perspective view. This is done using the Create Camera View tool. If you checked the Generate View After Add box, you'd be asked to pick the viewport to show the perspective view immediately after you placed the camera. Figure 8.17 shows the camera view applied to a viewport. The HIDE command was used on the perspective viewport.

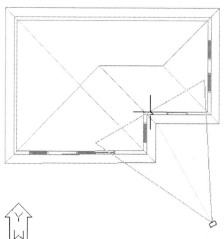

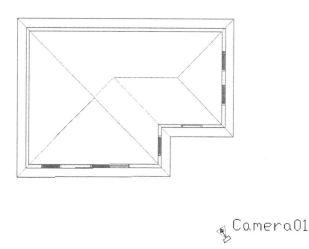

Figure 8.16 Sequence for adding a camera

Figure 8.17
Applying camera view
to viewport

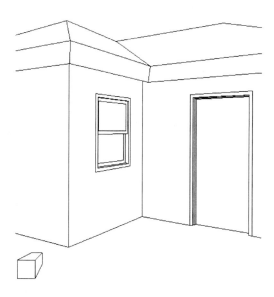

TIP: Creation Layer for Camera Object

If you're using the AIA layer standards set by the Desktop/Drawing Setup, the camera object is created on the A-Anno-Nplt layer and is blue. It's on a layer set not to plot.

Modifying the Camera Object

You can adjust the camera in several ways. The first is to use the Camera Properties tool, which gives you access to the insertion point and the lens size for the camera.

The second method is to use the camera object's grip points. If you select the camera object, the grips, as shown in Figure 8.18, appear. You can pick one and move it to a new location, thereby adjusting the camera properties. You can change the insertion point, the target point, and the FOV.

The last method of making modifications to the camera properties is to use the Adjust Camera View tool. When you've identified the camera to modify, an Adjust Camera Position dialog box similar to Figure 8.19 appears.

Using this dialog box you can adjust the position of the camera in incremental amounts. At the bottom of the dialog box are the increment values that you can set. The upper portion of the dialog box contains buttons that move the camera.

Usually, you will have the Auto View box checked so that when you make adjustments you can see the results on the screen. If the box is not checked, you have to use the Create Camera View tool to see the changes you made to the camera.

TIP: Apply Camera Changes to Viewport

When you make an adjustment to the camera properties, use the Create Camera View tool to apply the changes to the perspective viewport. The viewport will not update automatically.

TIP: Using DVIEW to Generate Perspective Views

If you want to create more complex perspective views that may require the rotation of the camera or the clipping out of objects, use the DVIEW command or 3D Orbit toolbar. Once you have the view you like, use the VIEW command to save it for later retrieval.

Figure 8.18   Grip points on the camera object

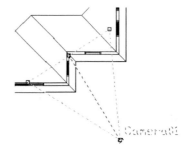

Figure 8.19 Adjust Camera Position dialog box

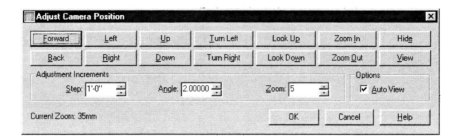

Creating a Video

You can create video animations of your model. The way to do this is to create a polyline path for the camera and one for the target and then set the camera to follow the paths. You can also use a point location for either the camera or the target.

Using a path for the camera and a point for the target creates the effect that the camera is moving around but looking at the same point. This is useful for creating a walk-around of a building.

Using a point for the camera and a path for the target creates the effect that the camera position is stationary, but the camera is swinging around to various target locations along the target path.

To create a video, switch to the Model layout and select the Create Video tool. Once you've picked your camera, you'll be presented with a dialog box similar to Figure 8.20.

The dialog box drop-down list boxes initially will be blank for the camera and the target path. In Figure 8.20, the dialog box shows that a circle was picked as the camera path and that a point was picked as the target location.

The Regen method is used to create the slide types. You can leave it as is (none) or use hide or different types of shade.

The Frames section controls the total number of frames and the number of frames per second.

The Options section allows you to see the camera movement using the Dry Run box. The Corner Deceleration box causes the frames to slow around sharp corners.

When you pick OK with the Dry Run box unchecked, you'll be asked to name the AVI file to be created. You'll also be asked for the type of compression. Once you have responded, the screen changes to show each frame as it is created and simultaneously writes to an AVI file. Once the file is done, you'll be asked if you want to run it now. If you respond Yes, the screen shows the animation. You can always play it later by double-clicking on the file in Windows® Explorer.

Figure 8.20 Create Video dialog box

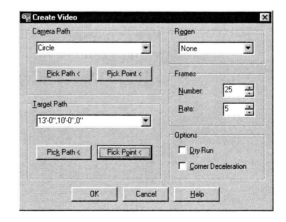

Hands-On: Creating a Camera View

In this exercise you'll add a camera and generate a camera perspective view. You'll also create an animation video using the camera.

1. Open file adtex8C, which contains a simple model of a house and a circular path to be used for camera movement. Save it as EX8C.

2. Activate the Work-3D layout and display the Perspectives toolbar.

Adding the Camera

3. Select the Add Camera tool and match your settings to those of Figure 8.21. Note that the eye level has been set to 10 feet. This will place the camera 10 feet above the 0 Z height. You'll later adjust the camera so that it's looking down.

Once you've altered the settings, place the insertion of the camera at 30′,−6′. Place the target point at 20′,6′. You'll then be asked to pick the viewport to display the camera view. Pick the left viewport. The screen should now look similar to Figure 8.22. Because the eye level was set to 10 feet, your view is mainly of the roof. In the next step, you'll adjust that.

Figure 8.21   Add Camera dialog box

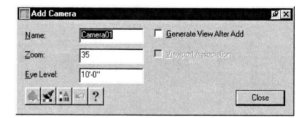

Figure 8.22   Results of applying the camera to the viewport

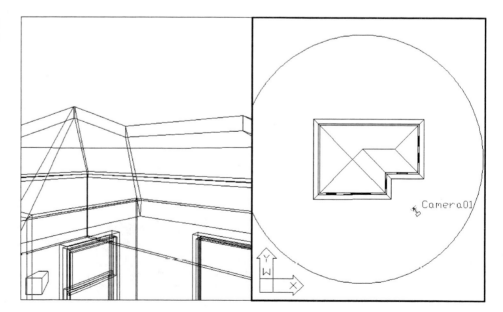

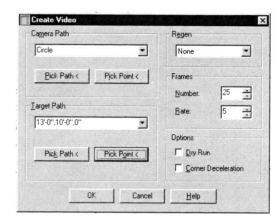

Figure 8.24   Create Video dialog box

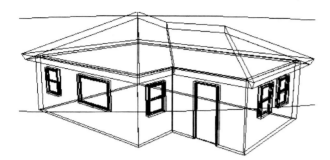

Figure 8.23   Adjusted camera view

Adjusting the Camera View

4.   Select the Adjust Camera View tool and pick the camera (if there's more than one) in the plan viewport. When the Adjust Camera Position dialog box appears, pick the Down button to lower the view. Experiment with the other buttons and create a view similar to Figure 8.23.

Creating a Video Animation

5.   Switch the Model layout and Zoom extents. Make sure the plan view is displayed.

6.   Select the Create Video tool and pick the camera (if there's more than one). For the Camera Path, use the Pick Path button and pick the circle. Enter Circle as the path name. For the Target Path, use the Pick Point button and enter 13′10′,0. See Figure 8.24 for the settings. Pick the OK button and enter EX8A as the AVI file name. Note where you're saving the file. Use Full Frames (Uncompressed) for the compressor type. When asked whether to play the video, answer Yes.

If you increase the total number of frames and increase the frame rate (frames per second), you'll get a smoother animation; the AVI file size, however, increases dramatically.

7.   Save your file as EX8C.

In a Nutshell

Once you've created your design/model, you can represent it with elevation, section, or perspective views.

You begin to create an elevation view by first creating an elevation object that is composed of any objects you select. You can then display the elevation object as an elevation view.

You create a section view in the same way as an elevation view, except that you section the model to create a section object.

Perspective views are created with the use of a camera object. The camera object behaves much like a real-world camera, allowing you to set the lens and to place the camera and the target to view. You can apply camera views to different viewports and create an animated video.

You have now gone through the basics of creating and viewing your design. The next stage is to create construction documentation.

 Testing... testing... 1, 2, 3

Fill-in-the-Blanks

1. In Architectural Desktop an elevation is an object derived from _____ and _____.

2. The elevation _____ defines the area that will be included in the elevation object, and the _____ is an indicator, telling you the direction in which the elevation line was created. They are created on the _____ layer and are colored _____.

3. You can use grips to adjust the section line's _____, _____, and _____.

4. The section object is created on the _____ layer and is colored _____. The edges of the section portion of the section object are created on the _____ layer and are colored _____.

5. You can create video animations of your model by creating one polyline path for the _____ and one for the _____.

Short Answers

6. It's often useful to place the section object a distance away from the original model so that _____
_____
_____.

7. It's important to give the camera a name so that _____
_____
_____.

8. You usually check the Auto View box so that _____
_____
_____.

True or False

9. The Corner Deceleration box causes the frames to slow around sharp corners.   T or F

10. A quick method of creating the four common elevation views is to create one elevation object that includes all the exterior objects.   T or F

 What?

1. What's the difference between an elevation view and a 3D model?

2. Describe the procedure for creating a viewing layout for an elevation object.

3. Explain the procedure you follow to create a video animation.

4. What are the differences between elevation and section objects?

5. What's the importance of the camera in perspective views?

6. Explain the difference between assigning a point to the camera and assigning a point to the target.

Let's Get Busy!

1. Take the floor plan design that you modified in Chapter 7, Let's Get Busy, and add a roof similar to Figure 8.25, then generate two elevation views as shown in Figure 8.26.

2. Take the floor plan to which you added the roof in Assignment 1 and fully section the view as shown in Figure 8.27.

3. Take the floor plan to which you added the roof in Assignment 1 and create a perspective view as shown in Figure 8.28.

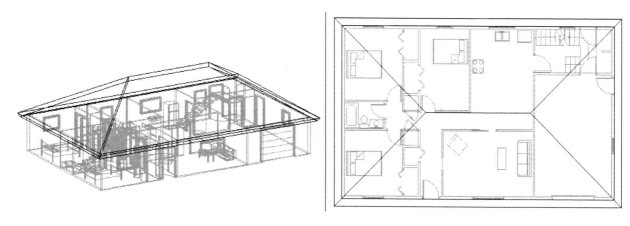

Figure 8.25   Floor plan with roof added

Figure 8.26 Two
elevation views

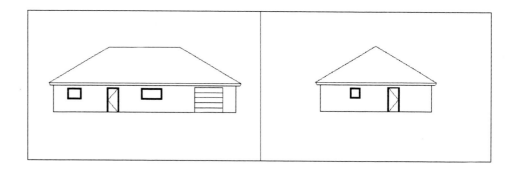

Figure 8.27   Section
view

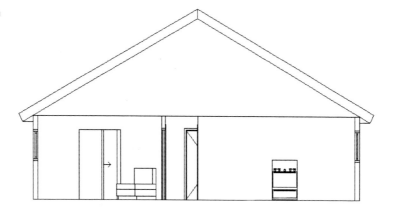

Figure 8.28
Perspective view

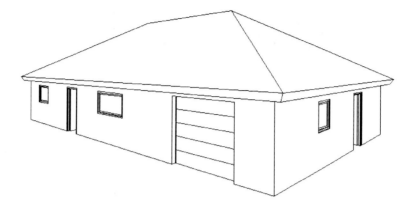

Chapter 9
Construction Documentation

The Great Oak

The oldest remaining oak in Sherwood Forest is not an architectural topic really, but the members used to support the tree combine nature and human input in a unique way. Until recently the soil around it was so trampled by hundreds of thousands of visitors that no moisture was getting to the roots. Now, with the soil protected, the tree is flourishing.

Key Concepts

- Working Drawings
- Dimensioning
- Drafting Symbols
- Scheduling
- Drawing Sheet Layout

Working Drawings

This chapter deals with the creation of construction documentation from your design. It explains the various methods of creating drawings and applying dimensions and annotations such as detail and elevation marks.

It's not the intent of this chapter to explain all the procedures that are required to create complete working drawings but to show you how to apply the Architectural Desktop commands in creating such drawings. The refinement of the documentation into complete working drawings involves the application of the standard AutoCAD drawing commands. The explanation of the standard AutoCAD drawing commands is not part of this text, but we will touch briefly on how they can be applied.

Dimensioning

To create a working drawing you need to be able to dimension the various features that make up the building. The best way to do this is to use the standard AutoCAD dimensioning commands. This gives you the greatest control over the dimensions.

Architectural Desktop has an automated feature for dimensioning walls. It does not always create the perfect dimensioning layout, but it can be used to speed up the dimensioning process.

Dimension Styles

Before you start dimensioning your building, you need to establish dimension styles. These styles control the appearance of the dimensions in your drawing. The method of creating and using dimension styles is the same in Architectural Desktop as it is using standard AutoCAD. Architectural Desktop creates a dimension style from which you can work.

TIP: Creation Layer for Dimensions

If you're using the AIA layer standards set by the Desktop/Drawing setup, the dimensions are created on the A-Anno-Dims layer and are pink.

Figure 9.1
Dimension Style
Manager dialog box

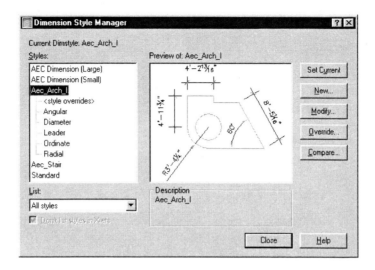

Selecting Dimension Styles from the Format pull-down menu displays the Dimension Style Manager dialog box as shown in Figure 9.1. When you set up your drawing using the Drawing Setup dialog box, found under the Desktop pull-down menu, you set the scale of your drawing. You normally do this when you start the project. This setting is added to the dimension style in the Overall Scale box under the Fit tab. You can change this setting at any time, and it will override the current dimension style settings.

You may want to review the Architectural Desktop dimension style to see if it matches your standards. Two items to review are the text style and the text height that you want in your drawings. They may be different from the Architectural Desktop values.

Text Styles

Most annotation content is set to use the current text style. To create a text style, use the standard AutoCAD STYLE command found under the Format pull-down menu. To allow for versatility with the text style you created, leave the text height of the style set to 0. This allows the height to change based on the dimension style you use or the annotation plot size, which is discussed later on.

Architectural Desktop creates a text style called RomanS. As with the dimension style, you may want to create your own. Just remember to make it current when you start adding text or dimensions.

Dimensioning Walls

Dimensioning Architectural Desktop walls is a very easy task. Because walls are intelligent objects, the information about their size and any openings contained within them is part of their properties. When you apply the dimension walls command to a wall, all the dimensional information is immediately extracted.

To dimension a wall, select the Dimension Walls tool from the Wall Tools toolbar. You'll be asked to select the wall to be dimensioned, followed by the location of the dimension line. You can then specify a second point to set the angle of the extension line, or type P to set the extension line perpendicular to the wall. Figure 9.2 shows the application of the wall dimension command.

You can also dimension a series of walls simply by selecting more than one wall at a time.

Figure 9.2
Dimensioning a wall

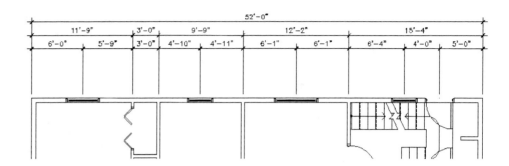

Opening Dimensions

If there are openings such as windows and doors that are part of the wall that is to be dimensioned, they will be dimensioned as well. Whether they are dimensioned from the center of the opening or from the outer frame of the opening is controlled by a setting found under the AEC DwgDefaults tab, located in the Options dialog box. Figure 9.3 shows the tab and the dialog box; Figure 9.4 shows both types of dimensioning.

Modifying Dimensions

The dimensions created using the Dimension Walls tool are standard AutoCAD objects, so you can modify them in any way. You can erase them individually or move them to new locations using their grip points. Figure 9.5 shows a wall dimensioned using the Dimension Walls tool and modified using the standard AutoCAD commands.

Figure 9.3 Options dialog box with the AEC DwgDefaults tab active

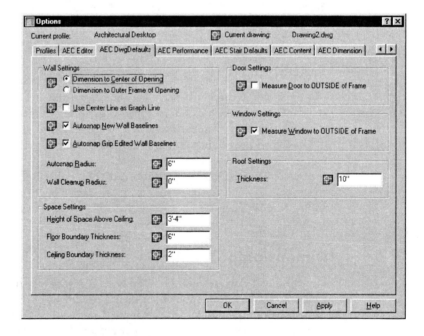

Figure 9.4
Dimensioning openings

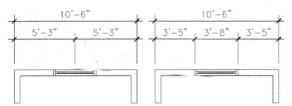

Figure 9.5
Modifying dimensions

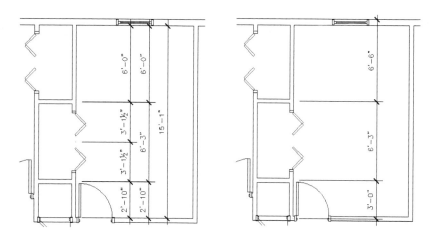

The dimensions are not intelligent and are not updated automatically when you make a change to your drawing. If you change the location or size of a feature, you must redimension it.

Hands-On: Adding Wall Dimensions

In this exercise you'll practice applying dimensions to an Architectural Desktop wall.

1.   Open file iaad3start, which is a copy of the template file that comes with Architectural Desktop. Save this drawing as EX9test.

Reviewing the Drawing Setup and Dimension Style

2.   Select Drawing Setup from the Desktop pull-down menu to display the Drawing Setup dialog box. Pick the Scale tab and observe the Drawing Scale. The scale is set to 1/4″=1′-0″. Look below in the Custom Scales box. It is gray, but the value 48 is displayed. This is the equivalent of 1/4″=1′-0″.

Now, look at the Annotation Plot Size. It is set to 3/32″. This is the scale of the text when it gets plotted. Usually you adjust the scale for the drawing and annotation at the start of the project, but you can make changes if you forget certain elements at the beginning.

Close the dialog box without making any changes.

3.   Select Dimension Style from the Format pull-down menu to display the Dimension Style Manager dialog box. Note the Aec_Arch_1 dimension style. It's created automatically when you use the Architectural Desktop template file to start a project. Note the <style overrides> label. Whenever you make changes to the Drawing Scale or Annotation Scale, the changes are made to the style overrides.

With the <style overrides> label highlighted, pick the Modify button. Pick the Text tab and observe the text height. It is set to 3/32″, which matches the scale set in the Drawing Setup dialog box. Also, notice the text style. It is set to RomanS. This was created by Architectural Desktop. You may want to create your own text style to use on your drawings.

Pick the Fit tab and observe the value in the Use overall scale box. It is set to 48 again to match the Drawing Setup.

4.   Open the Drawing Setup dialog box again and change the drawing scale to 1/2″=1′-0″. Note that the value in the Custom Scales box is now 24. Change the Annotation Scale to 1/4″. Pick the Apply button and close the dialog box.

5.   Open the Dimension Style Manager dialog box. Highlight <style overrides> and pick the Modify button. Open the Text tab and observe the text height. It did not change to match the 1/4″ in the Drawing Setup. You have to change this manually; it is not automatically changed. This is important to remember.

Open the Fit tab and observe the value in the Use overall scale box. It did change to 24 to match the Drawing Scale in the Drawing Setup dialog box.

Keep this in mind when you make changes: The drawing scale will change the overall scale in the style overrides, but the annotation scale will not change the text height.

6.   Save the file if you like.

Creating Wall Dimensions

7.   Open file adtex9A, which contains a series of walls to be used for applying dimensions. Save the file as EX9A.

8.   Switch to the Work-FLR layout and display the Wall Tools toolbar.

9.   Select the Dimension Walls tool and pick the wall at the top of the screen. Once you've picked the wall, press Enter to continue. When asked to pick a side to dimension, pick the location of the dimension line that will be closest to the wall (see Figure 9.6 for this location). When asked to indicate the second point, enter P. A series of dimensions similar to Figure 9.6 appear.

10.   Dimension the inside wall using the same method. See Figure 9.7 for the expected results.

11.   Using the standard AutoCAD commands, modify the interior wall dimensions so that they look like Figure 9.8.

12.   You're going to change the type of dimensioning on the outside wall from center to center, to edge of the openings.

Erase all the outside dimensions.

13.   Open the Options dialog box by typing OPTIONS on the command line. Scroll along the tabs and open the AEC DwgDefaults tab. Under the Wall Openings section check Dimension to Outer Frame of Opening. Pick the OK button to close the dialog box.

14.   Redimension the outer wall as before. The results should now look like Figure 9.9.

15.   Save your drawing as EX9A.

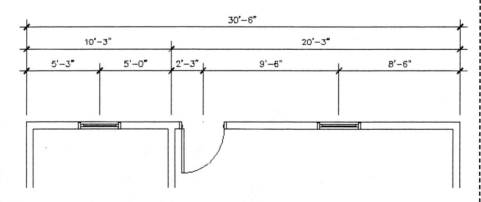

Figure 9.6   Placing the wall dimensions

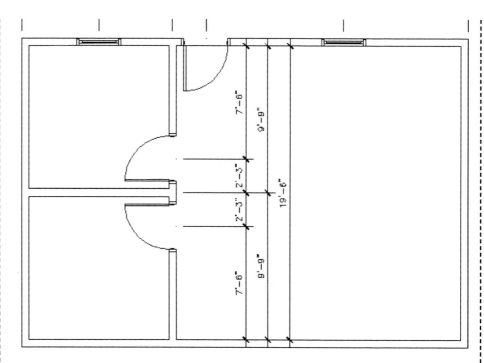

Figure 9.7   Dimensioning the interior wall

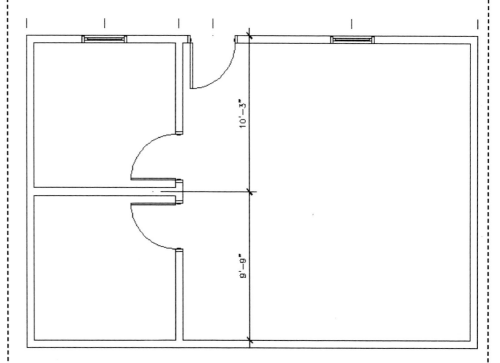

Figure 9.8   Modified interior wall dimensions

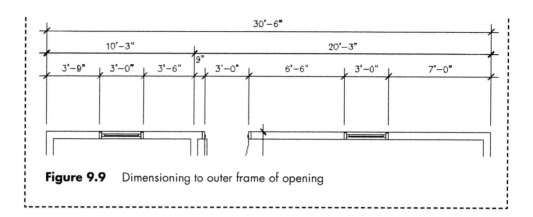

Figure 9.9   Dimensioning to outer frame of opening

Drafting Symbols

Architectural Desktop has a variety of annotation symbols that you can add to your draw-ings. Some of the types are Detail and Elevation Marks, Leaders, Break Marks, Revision Clouds, Title Marks, and Miscellaneous Symbols such as north arrows.

AutoCAD DesignCenter is used to import the various symbols into your drawing. When you select one of the annotation commands or tools, the DesignCenter is opened for use. The use of the DesignCenter was explained in Chapter 7, under Design Content. If you're unsure of how it functions, refer back to that chapter.

Most of the tools used to insert annotation symbols can be found on the documenta-tion toolbars. There is one for imperial and one for metric. Figure 9.10 shows the two toolbars.

Symbol Scales

Documentation symbols in Architectural Desktop are scale dependent. This means that they are scaled automatically when inserted based on the drawing setup. Usually the drawing settings are established when you start the drawing. To aid in the application of symbols, we will review the process.

If you select the Set Drawing Scale from the Documentation pull-down menu, the Drawing Setup dialog box appears (see Figure 9.11). Using this dialog box, you can set the scale for the drawing you're working on. This then affects the annotation symbols when you insert them. Note the Annotation Plot Size. This sets the text height from plotting annotations.

Also, note the Save As Default box. This is used if you want to establish a Drawing Setup that you want to use as the default. If you just want the settings to apply to the cur-rent drawing, do not check the box and pick the OK button.

Detail Marks

Detail marks are used to indicate an area on a drawing that will be detailed elsewhere. When you pick the Detail Marks tool, the DesignCenter appears showing you the vari-ous detail icons available (see Figure 9.12). You can place different types of area bound-aries, such as circular, rectangular, or custom shaped.

Figure 9.10   Documentation toolbars—Imperial and Metric

Figure 9.11
Drawing Setup dialog
box

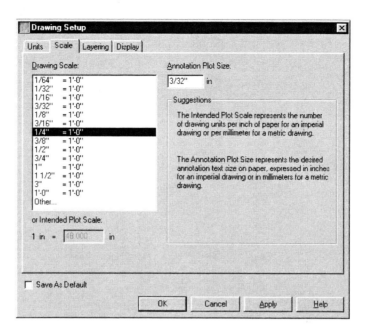

Figure 9.12
DesignCenter showing
detail icons and
application of circular
boundary

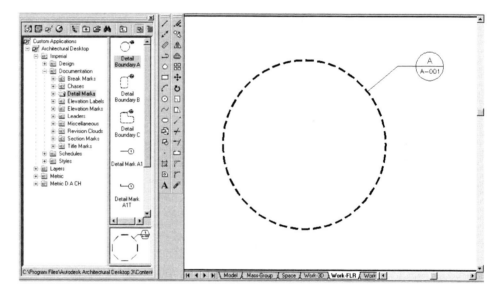

TIP: Creation Layer for Detail Marks

If you're using the AIA layer standards set by the Desktop/Drawing Setup, the
detail marks are created on the A-Detl-Iden layer and are green.

Circular Boundary To place a circular boundary and detail mark and boundary, pick
and drag the Detail Annotation A icon from the DesignCenter onto your drawing and
release the button. Specify the center of the detail circle and the radius. Then, indicate the
first point for the leader line and continue specifying points along the leader. Press Enter
when you have the desired leader. The Edit Attributes dialog box appears, as shown in
Figure 9.13. Fill in the Detail Number and the Sheet Number. Pick OK when you're fin-

Figure 9.13   Edit
Attributes dialog box

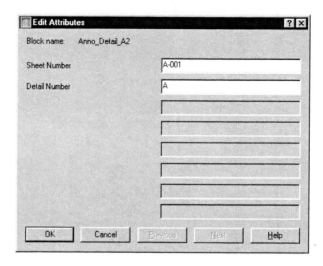

ished. The detail mark appears at the end of the leader at the same angle as the last section of the leader line.

Rectangular Boundary   To place a rectangular boundary and detail mark, select the
Detail Boundary B icon. To define the boundary area, pick the first corner and then the
opposite corner. The rest of the procedure is the same as for the circular boundary.

Custom Boundary   To place a custom-shaped boundary and detail mark, select the
Detail Boundary C icon. To define the boundary area, pick the first corner. You can then
adjust the boundary options such as the linetype. After making any adjustments, specify
points to define the shape of the boundary. Press Enter to close the boundary. Specify the
leader and mark identifications as before.

Detail Line   To place a detail line and mark, pick and drag one of the detail mark icons
onto the drawing. Then, pick the first and second points for the detail line. The first point
you pick will be the location of the detail balloon. You can adjust the properties of the line
and continue to pick points for the detail line. When you press Enter, the Edit Attributes
dialog box appears, as before. After entering the values and picking OK, you'll be asked to
specify on which side of the mark line you want the tail to be placed.

Elevation and Section Marks

Elevation marks are used to indicate where the elevation view is taken from, whereas section marks identify where the section view originated. When you pick the Elevation
Marks tool, the DesignCenter appears showing you the various elevation icons available
(see Figure 9.14). There are six types of elevation marks you can add to your drawing: A1,
A2, B1, B2, C1, and C2.

The application of the elevation mark is the same for each type. Pick and drag the elevation symbol onto the drawing. Specify the direction of the elevation mark, and alter its properties. Specify a second point, which is used to rotate the symbol. Enter the mark number in the

---

TIP: Creation Layer for Elevation and Section Marks

If you're using the AIA layer standards set by the Desktop/Drawing Setup, the
elevation and section marks are created on the A-Sect-Iden layer and are green.

Figure 9.14
DesignCenter showing
elevation icons

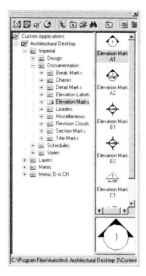

Edit Attributes dialog box and pick OK. You'll be asked if you want to add an AEC elevation object to the elevation mark. You do this if you want to create an elevation view from the placement of the elevation mark. The creation of elevation views was discussed in Chapter 8.

Section marks are applied in a similar manner.

Leaders

There are several styles of leaders that you can drag onto your drawing. Figure 9.15 shows some of the icons in the DesignCenter. Once the leader is dragged onto the screen, enter points as you would for any other leader, starting at the arrow and going toward the leader balloon. Press Enter when you've drawn the desired leader lines.

Break Marks

To draw a break line, drag the symbol onto the drawing and then specify the start and end points of the break line.

Break marks have the added ability to trim objects where they cross the break lines you create.

Figure 9.15
DesignCenter showing
leader icons

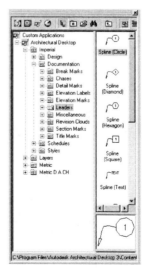

TIP: Creation Layer for Leader

If you're using the AIA layer standards set by the Desktop/Drawing Setup, the leaders are created on the A-Anno-Note layer and are pink.

TIP: Creation Layer for Break Marks

If you're using the AIA layer standards set by the Desktop/Drawing Setup, the break marks are created on the A-Anno-Sym layer and are green.

Revision Clouds

You can create revison clouds with three types of arcs: large, medium, or small. You can also add an identification tag, depending on the type of cloud you choose. Figure 9.16 shows some of the cloud icons and a drawn revision cloud.

Title Marks

Title marks are used to label views. Once you've placed a title mark, you can give it a number, title, and scale. Next, you specify the length of a polyline that is placed between the title and the scale.

TIP: Creation Layer for Revision Clouds

If you're using the AIA layer standards set by the Desktop/Drawing Setup, the revision clouds are created on the A-Anno-Revs layer and are light purple.

Figure 9.16
DesignCenter showing leader icons and a drawn revision cloud with I.D. tag

TIP: Creation Layer for Title Marks

If you're using the AIA layer standards set by the Desktop/Drawing Setup, the title marks are created on the A-Anno-Ttlb layer and are green.

Hands-On: Applying Drafting Symbols

In this exercise you'll practice applying the various drafting symbols that are available to you in Architectural Desktop.

1.   Open file adtex9B, which contains a simple floor plan with which to work. Save the file as EX9B.

2.   Make sure that the Work-FLR layout tab is active and that the Documentation - Imperial toolbar is visible.

Opening the DesignCenter

3.   Pick the Detail Marks tool from the Documentation - Imperial toolbar. The DesignCenter should appear at the left of your screen. It should automatically open the various Architectural Desktop folders until the Detail Marks folder is open. The various icons should be displayed to the right of the folder tree.

Adding a Detail Boundary and Mark

4.   Pick the Detail Boundary A icon to highlight it. Note that an enlarged version is displayed at the bottom of the DesignCenter. This is to show you the icon in a little more detail.

    Pick the icon you highlighted and drag it onto your drawing. Release the pick button. The command that places the detail mark now starts.

    The command asks you to specify where the center of the detail circle will be. Pick the endpoint of the upper-right corner wall. Enter a 3-foot radius for the circle. The next step is to create the leader line from the circle to the detail balloon (see Figure 9.17). Pick the first point to draw the leader on an angle and then pick a second point to draw the horizontal leader. After you pick the second point, press Enter to display the Edit Attributes dialog box. Enter A for the detail number and A-1 for the sheet number. Pick OK to continue.

    The text height in the balloon is controlled by the drawing scale and the annotation plot scale set in the Drawing Setup dialog box.

Figure 9.17   Adding a detail circle and mark

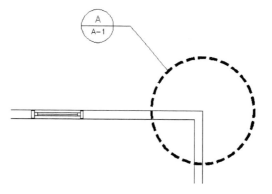

Adding a Revision Cloud

5.   Pick the Revision Clouds tool, and the DesignCenter displays the folder for revision clouds. Pick the icon for Small Arcs and Tag, and drag the icon onto your drawing. The command that places the revision cloud now starts.

See Figure 9.18 for the placement of the revision cloud. Start the cloud anywhere around its perimeter and then slowly drag the cursor around the perimeter in a counterclockwise direction. Every time you pass a distance equal to a small arc, the arc is drawn. As you complete the cloud, drag the cursor over the starting point and the cloud closes automatically. You may have to try the command more than once to get a feel for how the cloud is created.

You will then be asked to indicate the center of the identification tag (see Figure 9.18). The Edit Attributes dialog box appears. Enter 3 for the revision number.

Adding a Title Mark

6.   Using the Title Mark tool, create a title mark similar to Figure 9.19.

7.   Save the file as EX9B.

Figure 9.18   Adding a revision cloud

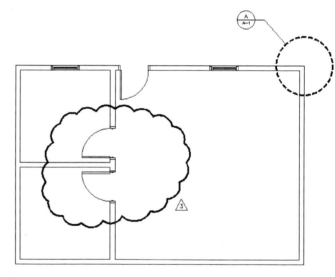

Figure 9.19   Adding a title mark

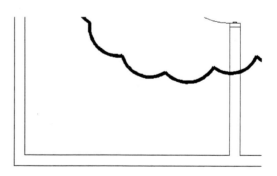

Scheduling

Schedule tables are created by attaching data tags to various objects in the drawing and then collecting the information contained in the tags. The information can be placed in a schedule table or exported to a separate file. The exported file can be in a TXT, tab-delimited format, an XLS (Excel), or CSV. This information can automatically update a schedule table. Figure 9.20 shows a schedule table and data tags attached to some doors.

Figure 9.21 shows the two Schedule toolbars, one for imperial and one for metric.

Schedule Tables Styles

The format of the schedule tables can be controlled in one of three ways: by using default schedule information style created by Architectural Desktop, by importing a schedule information style from another drawing, or by creating a custom style.

To access various Schedule Styles, select the Schedule Table Styles tool. A dialog box similar to Figure 9.22(a) appears. Use the File/Open pull-down menu item to open a drawing that contains schedule styles. Figure 9.22(b) shows the Open Drawing dialog box and Figure 9.22(c) shows the folder tree. Figure 9.23 shows the addition of the Schedules Table (imperial) drawing to the styles list. To use a style, simply drag it from one list to another.

Editing the Schedule Table Style

To control the way the table appears in your drawing, you'll want to edit the style. You may develop a set of standards establishing the way that your tables are created. At first it's easier to copy an existing style and edit it. To copy a style, highlight the style name in the Style Manager dialog box list and right-click to copy and right-click to paste the new copy. To edit a style table, highlight it, right-click, and pick Edit. The Schedule Table Style Properties dialog box appears, as shown in Figure 9.24(a). The various tabs control the appearance of the table. One particularly important tab is the Columns tab. It controls which items are created in the table and their order (see Figure 9.24(b)).

Figure 9.20
Schedule table and data tags

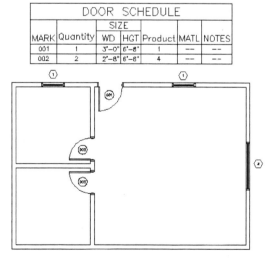

Figure 9.21
Schedule toolbars—imperial and metric

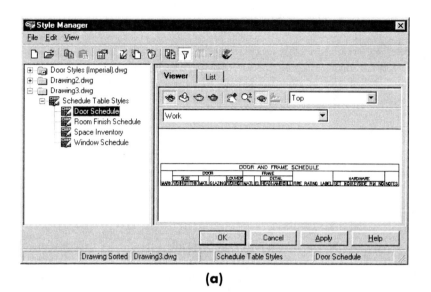

(a)

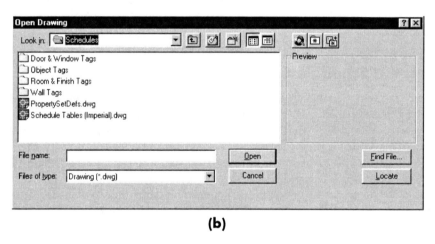

(b)

(c)

Figure 9.22   Style Manager showing schedule table styles

Figure 9.23   Style Manager showing the addition of the Schedules Table (imperial) drawing

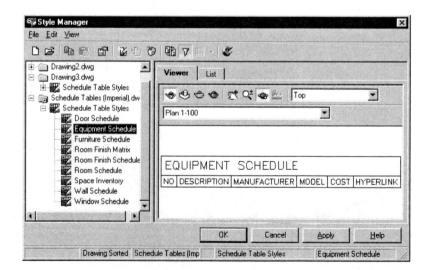

Figure 9.24   (a)
Schedule Table Style
Properties dialog box
and (b) Columns tab

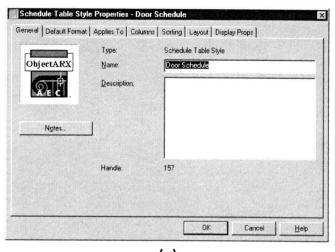

(a)

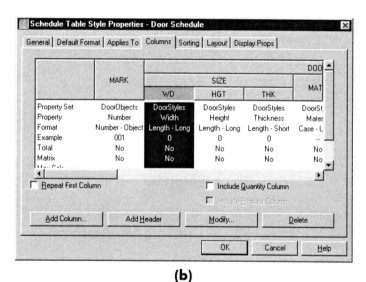

(b)

You can add columns and headers, or modify or delete them. If you move your cursor over a column, it will change into a hand symbol. You can then pick and drag a column into a new position. If you double-click on a column label, you can change its name.

Attaching Data Tags

Before you can create a table you have to attach data tags to the various objects in your drawing. The data tags contain all the information about the object to be compiled in the table. The DesignCenter is used to apply tags to your drawing. When you select one of the tag tools, the DesignCenter opens the folder that contains the appropriate tags for you to drag onto your drawing. There are four data tag types and four tools:

Door and Window Tags   Contains two tags, one for doors and one for windows

Room and Finish Tags   Contains three tags: one for room finish, one for room name and number, and one for a space tag

Object Tags

Contains seven tags that can be used to add data to any block object in your drawing. The seven are labeled Beam, Brace, Column, Equipment, Equipment (leader), Furniture, and Furniture (leader).

 Wall Tags

Contains two tags: Wall and Wall (leader)

To attach a tag, drag the icon from the DesignCenter onto the drawing and release the pick button. The command then starts by asking you to select the object to which to attach the data tag and then the location of the tag itself.

Once you do this, a dialog box appears for you to fill in or modify the data about the object. Figure 9.25 shows the dialog box for a window data tag. Each tag is given a new number, which is located at the bottom of the dialog box. You can give a new number to each object in your drawing, or you can edit the number so that it is the same for identical objects. Thus, when you create the table, only one line is created for the same objects, and their quantities can be totaled.

When placing the tag, you can change the symbol, add a leader (on some symbols only), or change the dimension style to be used.

Creating a Schedule Table

 To create a schedule table, select the Add Schedule Table tool, and a dialog box similar to Figure 9.26 appears. From this dialog box you can select the type of schedule to use from styles you have loaded into your drawing.

The Add New Objects Automatically box, if checked, adds objects to the table database as they're added to the drawing. The Automatic Update box, if checked, automatically updates the table that's placed in the drawing. This automatic update feature can reduce performance on very large, complex drawings. You can turn this box off and use the Update Schedule Table tool when necessary.

 TIP: Creation Layer for Schedule Tables

If you're using the AIA layer standards set by the Desktop/Drawing Setup, the schedule tables are created on the A-Anno-Legn layer and are light purple.

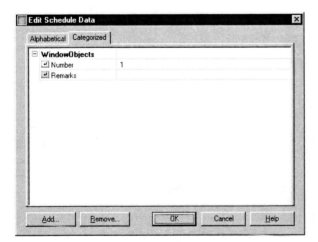

Figure 9.25   Edit Schedule Data dialog box for a window data tag

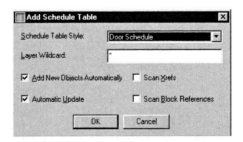

Figure 9.26   Add Schedule Table dialog box

TIP: Showing Objects That Are in a Schedule Table

To show which objects in your drawing are associated with a particular table, open the Documentation pull-down menu, and select Schedule Tables/Show Table Selection. Pick the border of the table, and the associated objects are highlighted.

When you pick OK to exit the dialog box, you are then asked to select the objects to be included in the table. Once you have done this, you'll be asked to place the table by its upper-left corner. You then can drag the lower-right corner to set the size of the table or press Enter to accept the default size. If you resize the table, the size of the text in the table is adjusted as well.

Updating the Schedule Table

You update the schedule table whenever you make changes to the objects associated with the table by using the Update Schedule Table tool.

Adding or Removing Objects

If you add objects to the drawing and you want to add them to an existing table, open the Documentation pull-down menu and select Schedule Tables/Selection/Add. You can then pick the objects to add to the table.

To remove objects from the table, open the Documentation pull-down menu and select Schedule Tables/Remove Table Selection.

You can also reselect all the objects to be included in a table. Open the Documentation pull-down menu and select Schedule Tables/Selection/Reselect.

Hands-On: Creating a Schedule Table

In this exercise you'll add data tags to some windows and doors and create two schedules.

1.   Open file adtex9C, which contains a simple floor plan that contains some windows and doors. Save the file as EX9C.

2.   Make sure that the Work-FLR layout tab is active and that the Schedule - Imperial toolbar is visible.

Adding Data Tags

3.   Pick the Door & Window Tags tool. The DesignCenter appears with the two icons for door and window tags displayed.

4.   Pick and drag the door icon onto the drawing and release the pick button. The command line then asks you to select a door to which to add the tag. Pick the top (exterior) door and place the tag as shown in Figure 9.27. You're not going to change any data, so pick OK when the dialog box appears.

You're asked to select another door to tag. Pick one of the interior doors and place the tag as shown in Figure 9.27. Pick the OK button to exit the dialog box.

Next, you're asked to pick another door. Pick the last interior door and place the tag. As before, pick OK to exit the dialog box. Press Enter to quit the command.

Figure 9.27 Tags added to the drawing

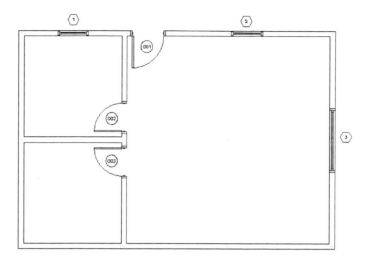

5. Pick and drag the window icon onto the drawing and release the pick button. As with the doors, tag all the windows (see Figure 9.27 for the placement of the tags).

Creating the Table

6. The first step in creating a table is to either create a table style or use an existing one. For this exercise, the style has already been created. Let's take a look at the styles in this drawing.

Select the Table Schedule Styles tool, and a dialog box similar to Figure 9.28 should appear. There are four styles contained in this drawing: Door Schedule, Ex9C Door Schedule, Ex9C Window Schedule, and Window Schedule. The Ex9C Door Schedule is a modified version of the standard Door Schedule. Some columns have been removed and a quantity column added. Close the dialog box. The Ex9C Window Schedule has the quantity column added as well.

7. Select the Add Schedule Table tool, and the dialog box should appear. Match your settings to those in Figure 9.29 and pick OK. Select the three door tags and press Enter. Place the upper-left corner of the table as shown in Figure 9.30 and press Enter to accept the default size for the lower-right corner. Use Zoom Extents to see the entire table. Most of the table is empty because you did not enter the

Figure 9.28 Style Manager dialog box

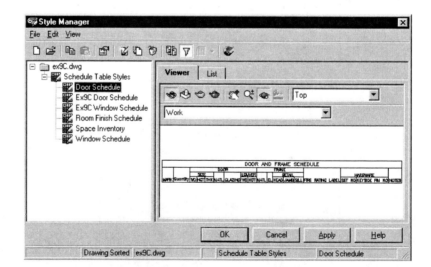

Figure 9.29   Add Schedule Table dialog box

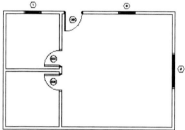

		DOOR AND FRAME SCHEDULE															
		DOOR						FRAME							HARDWARE		
		SIZE				LOUVER			DETAIL								
MARK	Quantity	WD	HGT	THK	MATL	GLAZING	WD	HGT	MATL	EL	HEAD	JAMB	SILL	FIRE RATING	LABEL	SET NO	KEYSIDE RM NO	NOTES
001	1	3'-0"	8'-8"	1 3/4"	--	—	0"	0"	--	—	—	—	--	—		--	—	--
002	1	2'-8"	8'-8"	1 3/4"	--	—	0"	0"	--	—	—	—	--	—		--	—	--
003	1	2'-8"	8'-8"	1 3/4"	--	—	0"	0"	--	—	—	—	--	—		--	—	--

Figure 9.30   The added table

information when attaching the tags. Note that there are three items numbered 001, 002, and 003. These correspond to the tags you added to the door objects.

Modifying a Table

8. In this step you're going to see how easy it is to change the style of an existing table.

Pick the table to highlight it and right-click to bring up the context menu. Select Table Properties from the menu. When the dialog box appears, pick the Style tab. Highlight the Ex9C Door Schedule and pick the OK button. The table in the drawing changed to a smaller modified version.

9. The two interior doors are the same doors, but they have different mark numbers. You are going to change the tag mark number of door 003 to 002.

Pick the 003 tab symbol next to the door to highlight it, and right-click to bring up the context menu. Select Edit Schedule Data, and the dialog box appears. Change the box number from 3 to 2 as shown in Figure 9.31, and pick OK.

Observe what happened to the door schedule. Because the automatic boxes were checked when the table was created, it is updated automatically when changes are made to objects in the drawing.

10. Create a window schedule using the Ex9C Window Schedule style and modify the data tags so that there are only two window types. Figure 9.32 shows the final table.

11. Save your file as EX9C.

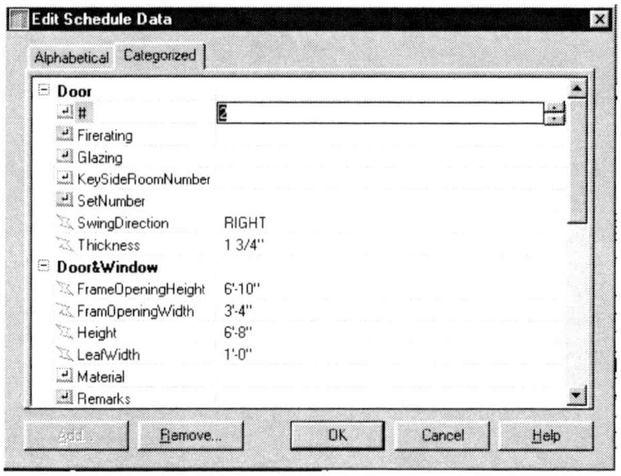

Figure 9.31 Edit Schedule Data dialog box

Figure 9.32 Window schedule

WINDOW SCHEDULE						
		SIZE				
MARK	Quantity	WIDTH	HEIGHT	TYPE	MATERIAL	NOTES
1	2	3'-0"	5'-0"	--	--	--
2	1	6'-0"	3'-0"	--	--	--

Drawing Sheet Layout

Laying out a drawing sheet in Architectural Desktop is no different than using standard AutoCAD. First, create a paper space layout using the LAYOUT command. Insert a titleblock/border at a scale of 1:1 on its own layer. Finally, create floating viewports using the MVIEW command to display your drawing objects.

The only extra element is the application of a display system to the viewports. Recall the introduction to display systems in Chapter 1. When you switch to a particular viewport, the representation of objects displayed changes depending on the display system applied to the viewport. You can assign viewport display configurations to the floating viewports to control what is displayed in each one. Remember that Select Display is found under the Desktop pull-down menu.

However, there are several things to keep in mind when creating the layout. What parts of the drawing can you keep dynamic and what parts will have to be static? The floor plan, for instance, is a dynamic part of the design. You can easily add walls and objects such as windows and doors, and the design automatically incorporates these items. When schedules are linked to objects in your drawing, they can be updated as well. However, some items, such as dimensions, are not dynamic. They do not change when you modify your drawing but remain static and have to be recreated when necessary.

You'll find through practice that not all your views can be dynamic; some details will have to be static just because of the nature of the details. To make your job a little easier, there are two ways to create static views from your dynamic model.

Static Views

Static views are views of your drawing that are not automatically updated when you make a change to the design. You can create static views from Architectural Desktop objects in one of two ways: quick slice and hidden line projection. They are not really views but objects created from a certain view or orientation.

Quick Slice extracts a polyline outline of a "slice" through one or more 3D objects. It produces a single polyline on the current layer. This can be useful in creating a sectioned profile through any object in your model. The polyline then can be used as a starting point to create a detail view. The QUICK SLICE command is found under the Desktop/Utilities pull-down menu.

Hidden Line Projection creates a "flat" 2D drawing from a 3D view of one or more objects. This tool can be extremely useful in creating elevation views. The created hidden line projection is a block that you can insert in the current drawing or use in another drawing. Once the block is inserted, you can explode it to refine and add details.

In a Nutshell

You have now covered all the basic elements that make up Architectural Desktop. You should be able to use Architectural Desktop to create conceptual designs, refine them with design development tools, and finally produce working drawings.

Becoming an expert in using Architectural Desktop takes time and plenty of practice, but now you should be ready to apply what you have learned to start you on your way to becoming that expert.

Architectural Desktop is a very powerful program and contains even more advanced techniques that are not within the scope of this book; some of these advanced techniques, however, are discussed in Appendix B to give you an idea of the possibilities.

 # Testing... testing... 1, 2, 3

Fill-in-the-Blanks

1. When you set up your drawing using the Drawing Setup dialog box, found under the Desktop pull-down menu, you set the _____ of your drawing. This is normally done when you _____ the project. This setting is added to the dimension style in the Overall Scale box under the _____ tab. You can change this _____ and it will override the current dimension style settings.

2. To allow for _____ with the text style you created, leave the text height of the style set to _____.

3. Because walls are _____ objects, the information about their size and any openings contained within them is part of their properties.

4. Architectural Desktop has a variety of annotation symbols, such as _____, _____, _____, _____ , _____, and _____.

5. Three different types of area boundaries include _____ , _____, and _____.

6. There are four data tag types. List these and label the tags that are found under each of the four.

a. _____   b. _____   c. _____   d. _____

   (1)_____   (1)_____   (1)_____   (1)_____

   (2)_____   (2)_____   (2)_____   (2)_____

                      (3)_____   (3)_____

                                              (4)_____

Multiple Choice

7. There are how many types of revision clouds?

   a. one

   b. three

   c. five

   d. seven

   e. nine

8. Once you've placed the title mark, you can give it

   a. a number, a setting, and a designation.

   b. a number, title, and scale.

   c. a scale and a location.

   d. all the above

   e. a and b

True or False

9. The only extra element in Drawing Sheet Layout in Architectural Desktop is the application of display systems to the viewports.   T or F

10. Hidden Line Projection creates a 3D view from a "flat" 2D drawing of one or more objects.   T or F

What?

1. Explain the purpose of a detail mark. Do the same for an elevation mark and a leader line.
2. What is the procedure for dimensioning walls in Architectural Desktop?
3. Describe the procedure for adding a scheduling table to a drawing.
4. What is the purpose of a static view?
5. Describe the creation of a revision cloud. What is its purpose?

Let's Get Busy!

1. Using the tools presented in this chapter, create a working drawing of the floor plan created in the previous Let's Get Busy. Add dimensions, annotations, and window and door schedules.

Appendix

Advanced Applications

This appendix introduces you to some of the advanced applications that Architectural Desktop has to offer. These applications are beyond the normal scope of this book, but we wanted to make you aware of the possibilities. This appendix gives you an overview of the features.

Display Systems

As explained in earlier chapters, the display system controls how objects are displayed in a designated viewport. Each object in Architectural Desktop is made up of various components. The components may be two-dimensional for plans and elevations and three-dimensional for isometric or perspective views. When a display system is assigned to a viewport, it effectively controls which of these components are visible and which are hidden from view.

The following is the procedure that Architectural Desktop uses to determine if an object is displayed or not:

1. **Get the display configuration.**

   If you're drawing the object in a paper space viewport and a display configuration is attached to the viewport, then the display configuration is used. However, if you're drawing an object in model space, then the default display configuration is used.

2. **Get the display representation set from the display configuration.**

   If the display configuration is view-direction-dependent, get the view direction of the viewport. Get the display representation set that matches the view direction. If the display configuration is fixed, use that display representation set.

3. **Get the current viewing direction.**

   If the display configuration doesn't have a fixed viewing direction, then get the viewing direction from the viewport.

4. **For every display representation that is selected (on) in the display representation set, do the following:**

   Specify the display representation to draw.

   When the display representation draws, the display representation uses display properties defined for the particular object. The display properties that are used depend on whether any display properties have been attached as overrides. The display representation first looks for display properties on the object being drawn. If the display properties are not there, then it looks at that object's style properties (if it has a style). If the object does not have a style, it uses the system default display properties. The object then draws its geometry using the display properties found. The viewing direction may be used to determine what graphics are drawn (as in the case of multiview blocks).

Default Display Representations by Object

Each object type has a default display representation set applied to it based on the display configuration. This is the first level of display control and is already set for you in the pro-

Figure B.1 Display Manager dialog box with Representations by Objects folder open

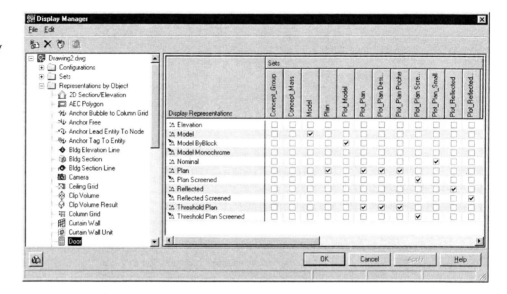

totype. If you want to check what is being used, or if you want to modify the display representation that's applied to an object, you can select Display Manager from the Desktop pull-down menu. A dialog box appears as shown in Figure B.1. If you open the Representations by Object folder, you can highlight an object type and have access to the representation sets.

Display Representation Sets

Display Representation Sets are the second level of display control. They are collections of display representations, grouped under set names. Figure B.2 shows the Display Manager with the Sets folder open. This is accessed from the Desktop/Display Manager pull-down menu. You can edit a display set by highlighting it.

Display Configurations

Display Configurations are the final level of display control. They contain one or more display representation sets. The Display Configurations are what you apply to a viewport. To access the Display Configurations dialog box, select Desktop/Display Manager and

Figure B.2 Display Manager with the Sets folder open

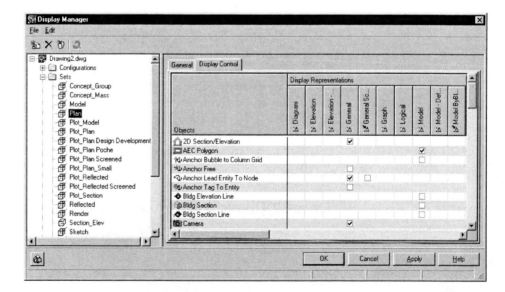

Figure B.3 Display Manager with the Configurations folder open

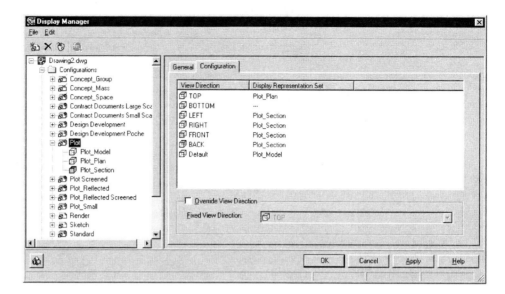

Figure B.4 Display Manager showing properties of a display set

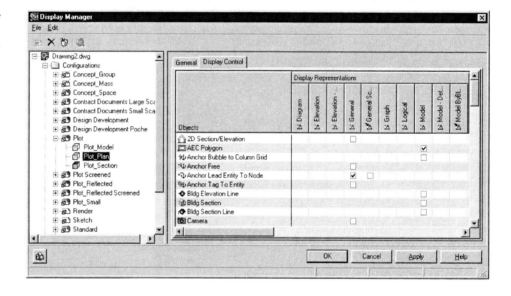

open the Configurations folder. A dialog box similar to Figure B.3 appears. If you're using the Architectural template file, the configurations are already created. If you highlight a configuration, the view dependencies are listed. If you open a configuration and highlight a set, its properties are listed as shown in Figure B.4.

Layer Manager

The Layer Manager is used to organize, sort, and group layers. Layer naming uses a preset standard, so that all the layers use the same format for naming. The concept is to group together similar layers to make organizing a complex multilayer drawing easier.

To access the Layer Manager dialog box, select Desktop/Layer Management/Layer Manager. A dialog box similar to Figure B.5 appears.

The following is a list of the icons along the top of the dialog box and their purpose:

Figure B.5   Layer
Manager dialog box

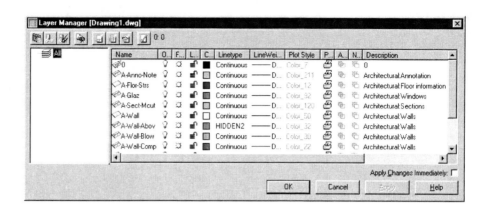

	Layer Standards	Sets the standard to be used for layer naming; by default it is set to AIA long format.
	Layer Key Styles	Displays a dialog box that contains the various key styles that are loaded into the drawing. A layer key is a map between an AEC object that you draw on screen and a defined layer.
	Layer Key Overrides	Overrides the layer style.
	Snapshots	Displays a dialog box that allows you to take a "snapshot" of the status of the layers. You can assign a name to the snapshot. You can later restore the condition of the layers by restoring the snapshot.
	New Layer	Allows you to create a new layer using a layer standard layer key.
	New Filter Group	Allows you to filter what layers you want to access. You can save the filter by name so that you can later recall the filter to use over again.
	New User Group	Allows you to create groups of layers, combined under a group name. Once you have created a group, you can then add what layers you want in the group by picking objects in the drawing.
	Current Layer	Sets the currently highlighted layer current to draw on.

Anchors

The purpose of anchors is to attach an AEC object to another "parent" object in the drawing. In this way the anchored object travels with the parent object. You can release anchored objects so that they're free to move on their own. There are five types of anchors: curve anchors, leader anchors, node anchors, cell anchors, and volume anchors. Figure B.6 shows the Anchors toolbar.

Curve Anchors

Curve anchors attach objects to the base curve of other objects. It should be noted that the curve object can be straight. The types of objects you can anchor to are arcs, circles, mass elements, polylines, roofs, and walls.

Figure B.6   Anchors
toolbar

To anchor an object to a curve, select the Curve Anchor tool. Use the AT option to attach the object to the curve.

Leader Anchors

Leader anchors attach objects to nodes on layout curves, layout grids, and layout volumes, with the use of a leader. In this way the object is separated from the layout object by the leader line. Layout objects are explained later in this appendix.

To anchor an object to a layout object, select the Leader Anchor tool. Use the A option to attach the object to the layout object.

Node Anchors

Node anchors attach objects directly to nodes on layout curves, layout grids, and layout volumes, with the use of a leader. Layout objects are explained later in this appendix.

To anchor an object to a layout object, select the Node Anchor tool. Use the A option to attach the object to the curve. You can use the Copy option to copy the object to each node on the layout object. When using the Copy option, select a node on the layout object.

Cell Anchors

Cell anchors attach objects to cells (center of grid bays or volumes) on layout grids and layout volumes. Layout objects are explained later in this appendix.

To anchor an object to a layout object, select the Cell Anchor tool. Use the A option to attach the object to the layout object.

Volume Anchors

Volume anchors attach objects to volumes on layout volumes. Layout objects are explained later in this appendix.

To anchor an object to a layout object, select the Volume Anchor tool. Use the A option to attach the object to the layout object.

Layout Curves and Grids

Layout curves and grids are used to assist you in establishing relationships among objects. There are three types of layouts: layout curves, 2D layout grids, and 3D volumes. Figure B.7 shows the Layout Tools toolbar.

Layout Curve

A layout curve is used to anchor objects along a path (see Figure B.8). You can use walls, mass elements, roofs, lines, arcs, circles, ellipses, polygons, polylines, and splines as layout curves. The first step is to place anchor nodes along the path. Objects can then be attached to the nodes. There are three methods of placing nodes along the path: manual, repeat, and space evenly. Manual allows you to specify the location of each object to anchor. Repeat

Figure B.7 Layout Tools toolbar   **Figure B.8** Layout curve and nodes

allows you to specify the start and end offset distance and the distance between the nodes. Space evenly allows you to specify the start and end offset distance and the number of nodes to be placed. They're then spaced evenly over the length of the path.

To generate a layout curve, select the Add Layout Curve tool. You'll be asked to select the appropriate object to use as a layout curve and then the node placement method. Depending on the method, you'll be asked the start and end offset distance and the location of the nodes.

When the nodes have been placed, use the Node Anchor tool item to select the object to attach to a node and the layout curve node to which it is to be attached.

2D Layout Grids

Layout grids are used to arrange objects in a 2D grid pattern, which can be rectangular or radial. Once a grid is created, you can anchor objects to the intersection of the grid lines (nodes) or to the center of the grid bays (cells).

To create a layout grid, select the Add Layout Grid (2D) tool.

3D Layout Volumes

Layout volumes are used to arrange objects in a 3D rectangular grid pattern. Once the grid is created, you can anchor objects to the intersection of the grid lines (nodes) or to the center of the grid bays (volumes).

To create a layout grid, select the Add Layout Volume (3D) tool.

Masking Blocks

A masking block is a 2D object that is used to hide parts of an object in a 2D view. Its purpose is to clean up or alter objects in your drawings by hiding from view portions of the objects covered by the 2D masking shape. The procedure involves creating a masking block and then attaching one or more AEC objects to it, to mask parts of the AEC objects.

Defining the Masking Block

The first step in creating a masking block is to draw a closed 2D polyline. This shape will be used as the mask. Then define the masking block by opening the Mask Blocks dialog box (Desktop/Mask Blocks/Mask Block Definitions pull-down menu). Create a new masking block by right-clicking on the Mask Blocks heading and give it a unique name. To assign a closed polyline to the masking block, right-click on the new masking block, pick Set From, and select the previously drawn closed polyline.

The masking object must be at the same elevation as the objects to be masked. If you are masking walls, the masking block must be located at the base of the wall.

Masking an AEC Object

To mask an AEC object, select Desktop/AEC Masking/Attach Objects to Mask. Select the masking block and then select the AEC object that you want to mask. Finally, identify the view that will be used. The masking object hides any portion of the AEC object it covers.

Curtain Walls and Window Assemblies

A curtain wall object provides a skeletal grid work to assemble other objects such as windows and doors. The common application is to form complex wall systems, such as store fronts, into a single object.

The curtain wall object is composed of vertical and horizontal grids. Each cell in a grid can contain a panel infill or another object such as window or door. A panel infill represents a basic material.

Curtain wall objects are initially designed as a style and then inserted into the drawing or converted from a layout grid into a curtain wall. Figure B.9 shows the Curtain Walls toolbar and Figure B.10 shows the addition of a curtain wall object to a drawing.

If you pick the Curtain Wall Styles tool, a Style Manager dialog box similar to Figure B.11 appears. From the style list, you can create a new curtain wall style or copy or modify an existing style. If you edit an existing style, a dialog box similar to Figure B.12

Figure B.9   Curtain Walls toolbar

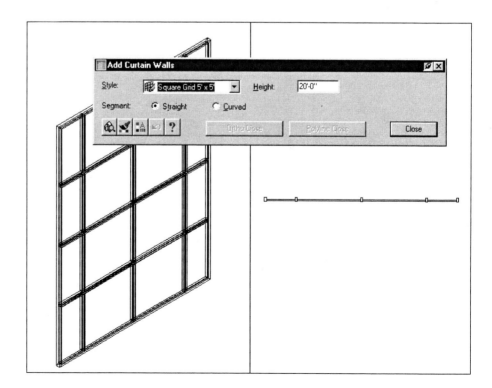

Figure B.10   Add Curtain Walls dialog box and curtain wall object

Figure B.11 Style Manager showing curtain wall styles

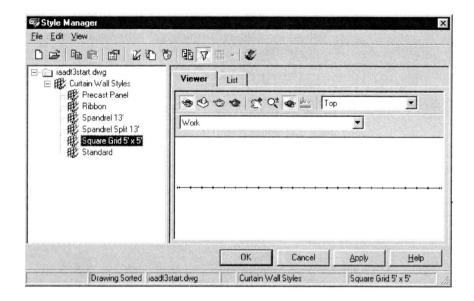

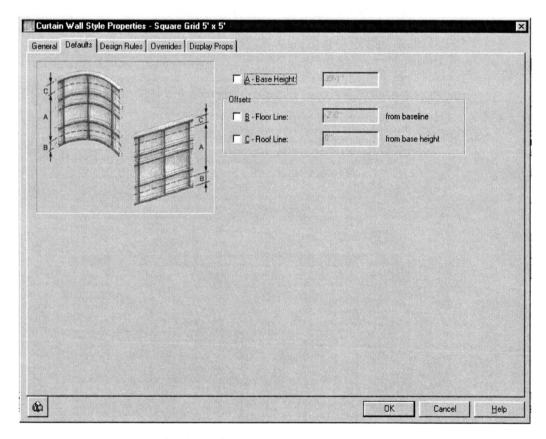

Figure B.12 Curtain Wall Style - Defaults Tab

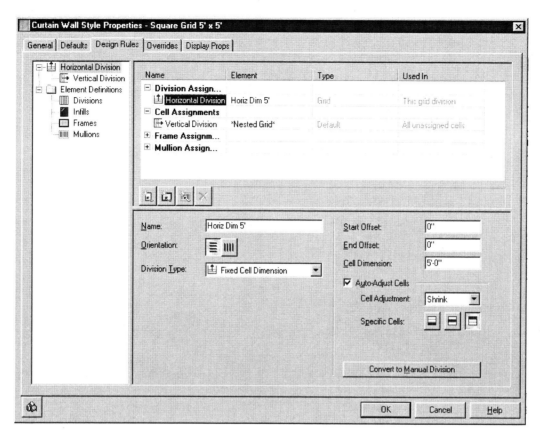

Figure B.13   Curtain Wall Style Properties dialog box with Design Rules tab active

appears. Under the Defaults tab, you can make some size changes. The Design Rules tab is used to create a grid and to establish the interior elements. Refer to Figure B.13.

Another object type contained in the Curtain Walls toolbar is the curtain wall unit. Curtain wall units are very similar to curtain walls except that the grid cells can only contain panel infills, not objects.

Window Assemblies

A windows assembly object is very similar to a curtain wall object in its creation and application. It is composed of a skeletal grid into which you can insert panels or window or door objects.

To add or manipulate windows assemblies, use the Doors - Windows - Openings toolbar as shown in Figure B.14. Figure B.15 shows the addition of a window assembly to a wall.

Figure B.14   Doors - Windows - Openings toolbar

Figure B.15 Add
Window Assemblies
dialog box and Window
Assembly object

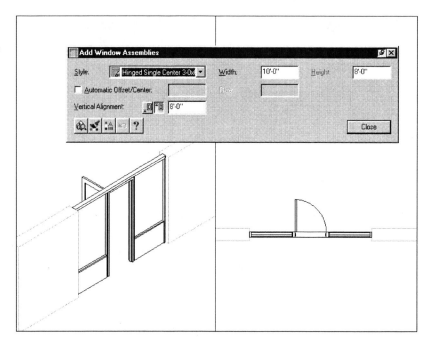

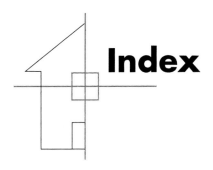

Index